Partha & Sikha
May stars shine on you
Best wishes

10/6/09

Why Astrology is Science:

Five Good Reasons

Tapan Das, PhD. P.Eng.

iUniverse, Inc.
New York   Bloomington

Cover design by Tapas Das

iUniverse books may be ordered through booksellers or by contacting:

iUniverse
1663 Liberty Drive
Bloomington, IN 47403
www.iuniverse.com
1-800-Authors (1-800-288-4677)

Because of the dynamic nature of the Internet, any Web addresses or links contained in this book may have changed since publication and may no longer be valid. The views expressed in this work are solely those of the author and do not necessarily reflect the views of the publisher, and the publisher hereby disclaims any responsibility for them.

ISBN: 978-1-4401-3371-8 (sc)
ISBN: 978-1-4401-3372-5 (ebook)
ISBN: 978-1-4401-3373-2 (hc)

Library of Congress Control Number: 2009927275

Printed in the United States of America

iUniverse rev. date: 5/18/2009

This book is dedicated to my parents,

Sristi Dhor Das

and

Sushama Das

Acknowledgments

I have been interested in astrology since I was a boy because of my family background. But as I grew older and started studying science and engineering, I was becoming increasingly concerned with the way this ancient science was being presented and practiced. However being extremely busy in my working life, I could not afford to spend any time in pursuing my interest in astrology. After my retirement from full-time work, I devoted all my time in researching in astrology, astronomy, cosmology, biofield, and alternative medicine to establish a solid scientific explanation for astrology. I spent such long hours at home and libraries to pursue my work, that my wife Samira was wondering whether I had really retired from full-time work. However, she understood my passion and encouraged me to pursue it. I am extremely grateful to Samira for her understanding and encouragement. I am thankful to my son Tapas for providing the book cover design, few diagrams, and helpful suggestions I am also thankful to my daughter Neeta for encouraging me to write the book. Finally, I am thankful to the editorial staff of iUniverse for editing my manuscript.

Contents

Preface

The purpose of this book is to explain astrology as science—social science. The scientific community considers astrology as a pseudoscience or superstition, which astrologers vehemently challenge. But when the astrologers are asked to name the branch of science to which astrology belongs, they cannot offer a definite answer.

Astrology started as a subject intimately connected to astronomy. The history of astrology is similar to the history of astronomy. The two subjects parted company after Nicolaus Copernicus postulated that the Sun—not Earth—is the center of the solar system. But astrology continued with the belief that Earth is the focus of the solar system and the universe. According to astrology, the planets and celestial objects indicate the course of human life on Earth.

This book gives five good scientific reasons why astrology is a science and explains each reason in detail—I have researched this subject for five years. I earned a master's degree and a doctorate degree in electronic engineering and have worked in the field for thirty-five years. My interest in astrology, however, is strong, and I am disappointed that astrology is seen as a pseudoscience by the scientific community. After retiring from my job, I devoted all my time to research on astrology, with the sole intention of explaining astrology on scientific basis. I have published six articles on this topic in the *International Society of Astrology Research (ISAR)* and

Research in Astrology with Media in Science (RAMS), and Journal of the Mindshift Institute.

This book is targeted for three groups of readers: the scientific community, the astrology community, and the general public.

A full chapter is devoted to each good reason, and each reason is explained using scientific data, collected from the work of experts in the field, and then making logical conclusions for the reason. A brief background of astrology is given for the benefit of the scientific community and general public.

The general public may be interested in astrology because it predicts the future. One asks an astrologer a specific question about one's future, and the astrologer gives a specific answer to that question. After reading this book, the reader will understand that astrology can explain the past and present and outline the future, but it cannot answer a specific question. Astrologers predict how the stars and planets will indicate the positive or negative aspects of a person's life. If proper actions are taken by the individual, then favorable results can be achieved and unfavorable conditions can be avoided.

After reading this book, the scientific community will begin to see astrology in a new perspective. Astrology is based on the statistical analysis of data of the positions of stars and planets in the sky at a certain time, coincident with the characters of people born at that time and the events at Earth at that time. Astrology analysis results are not certainty but probability. There is no definite answer to a specific question; the answer is based on probability.

Social science studies the way in which economics, education, culture, religion, political system, etc., are related to the social life of individuals and human groups. The study involves intense statistical analysis to conclude results. Astrology studies the relationship between the celestial objects and human life. Thus, astrology is another branch of social science, extending the area of social science to celestial objects, using statistical analysis. Astrology is not competing with astronomy or physics or any other branch of natural science or mathematical science.

For astrologers, this book provides a new directive. Astrologers should avoid providing answers to any specific future-related question; instead, they should predict the future as favorable or unfavorable conditions for their clients; how the positions of the stars and planets in the charts of the clients indicate conditions of wealth or poverty, joy or sorrow, conflict or amity, and danger or peace. With this kind of prediction, clients can take appropriate action to achieve success and avoid any downfall. Astrologers should also share their knowledge and experience, hence constantly improving and modifying the subject of astrology. Astrologers, psychologists, and alternative medicine practitioners should share their knowledge for mutual benefit.

To my knowledge, there is no such book currently published that places astrology as a social science with fully explained good reasons.

Introduction

That we can now think of no mechanism for astrology is relevant but unconvincing. No mechanism was known, for example, for continental drift when it was proposed by Wegener. Nevertheless, we see that Wegener was right, and those who objected on the grounds of unavailable mechanism were wrong.

—Carl Sagan

Is astrology a science? Astrology and astronomy are historically one and the same discipline, but they gradually started separating in the seventeenth century and were completely separated by the eighteenth century. Astronomy and its subfields, astrophysics and cosmology, attempt to understand the formation, function, and physics of the planets, stars, and galaxies of the universe. Astrology, on the other hand, studies and correlates the impact of celestial events on human life and earthly events.

Astrology made its strongest upswing in popularity in all of history in the early 1930s, when British astrologer R. H. Naylor created the first daily newspaper horoscope column. Soon, every newspaper had such a column, and every town had several practicing astrologers.

In spite of the attempt of a knock-out blow to astrology by the scientific community, the popularity of astrology is ever increasing. The well-publicized anti-astrology statement in the *Humanist* magazine of September 1975, signed by 186 scientists, including nineteen Nobel Laureates, had little effect on the popularity of astrology. The paradoxical result is that the heyday of astrology was not during the benighted Middle Ages, when the average person was sunk deep in ignorance and superstition and kept there by illiteracy and the rarity of books. Rather, the popularity of astrology is ever increasing now, when most citizens presumably know the basic facts of astronomy from space-probe photos in the daily newspapers and on TV that show that the other planets are more or less similar to Earth and not mystical god-fires in the sky. At the present time, at least 90 percent of all Americans under age thirty are said to know their Sun sign. How many people know their blood type? Or the name of the Secretary of State? Or Newton's three laws of motion?

Physics and cosmology, so far, have dealt with inanimate objects. These branches of science consider that matter and human body consist of molecules, atoms, and subatomic particles. In the twentieth century, we saw an exponential advancement of science, engineering, and technology with the invention of automobiles, television, telephones, cell phones, the Internet, airplanes, satellites, etc. People were bombarded with technology gadgets. Man landed on the Moon. We send space missions to explore the universe, but still, science has not addressed the life force in humans, animals, and plants.

> *Albert Einstein was once asked by a friend, "Do you believe that absolutely everything can be expressed scientifically?"*
>
> *"Yes, it would be possible," he replied, "but it would make no sense. It would be description without meaning—as if you described a Beethoven symphony as a variation in wave pressure."*
>
> —Ronald W. Clark, *Einstein: The Life and Times*

There is a subtle energy in the music that creates the melody and tune in music. This energy is unknown to science. There is an energy force in humans, animals, and plants. This energy force was called *prana* or *chi* in ancient culture; this is the energy force that makes the difference between a dead body and a living person. With all available scientific techniques and gadgets, scientists will never be able to bring back life into a dead body. Scientists are not able to create the energy force called prana or chi. Scientists now should focus on researching the area of life energy force: its function, attributes, origin, and compositions.

Medical science mainly concentrates on the body, body parts, and organs. Diseases that caused pandemics and mass death can now be cured by antibiotics and vaccines. Physicians perform surgical operations that were never thought possible in an earlier age. However, medical science is still unaware of life energy flowing through the body and does not consider the unison of body, mind, and life energy that works in balanced harmony to keep a healthy body and mind.

Astrology could play a major role in the study of the human mind. Carl Jung's famous quote about astrology is as follows:

> *Obviously astrology has much to offer psychology, but what the latter can offer its elder sister is less evident. So far as I judge, it would seem to me advantageous for astrology to take the existence of psychology into account, above all the psychology of the personality and of the unconscious.*

People sometimes ask astrologers if they are going to make lots of money, enjoy good health, become famous, or have a glamorous love affair—they want specific answers to specific questions:

- Am I getting a promotion this year?

- Is my daughter getting married this year?

- Is my son going to pass his exam?

- Will my stocks go up?

- Are we going on a cruise?

- Am I going to have a son?

These are all specific, material questions. Astrology and one's horoscope illuminate the path of a person's life, showing the outline of the future. Astrology never indicates that "this cannot be done" or "you are completely of luck." Rather, it shows our strengths and weaknesses, what can be done, and how and when.

Stars incline, but they do not compel.

—*Horoscopes, Your Daily Future and Fortune.*
Greenwich, England

Stars and planets each have a different influence on our lives, depending on their position in their signs and heavenly houses. The energy from them causes us to be bright or dull, hasty or slow, calm or nervous. They bring conditions of joy or sorrow, conflict or peace, anger or calm. All these cosmic forces shape our thoughts, which in turn direct our actions.

If we are warned that we are prone to rash actions due to the influence of certain planets, then we can hold a check on our emotion and avoid rash action and catastrophic results. If we know that the position of the planets give a favorable condition, then we can take advantage of it by proper action. This is how astrology can help us without giving specific answers to specific questions.

This book gives five good reasons why astrology is science:

1. Astrology is based on statistical analysis.

2. Astrology is social science.

3. Astrology is linked with alternative medicine.

4. Astrology is explained by cosmic energy and biofield.

5. The basis of astrology is similar to quantum mechanics.

I have carried out intense research for the last five years to develop these reasons, spending countless hours in the library, studying and collecting the scientific work of experts in these areas. I have published some of my work in three journals, as mentioned in the preface. All five reasons are explained in clear detail in chapters three to seven. A brief overview of astrology is given in chapter two.

> *Courteous Reader, Astrology is one of the most ancient Sciences, held in high esteem of old, by the Wise and the Great. Formerly, no Prince would make War or Peace, nor any General fight in Battle, in short, no important affair was undertaken without first consulting an Astrologer.*

> —Benjamin Franklin
> *Poor Richards Almanac 1751*

Chapter 1
Basics of Astrology

The cosmos is a vast living body, of which we are still parts. The sun is a great heart whose tremors run through our smallest veins. The moon is a great nerve-center from which we quiver forever. Who knows the power that Saturn has over us, or Venus? But it is a vital power, rippling exquisitely through us all the time.

—*D.H. Lawrence,* Apocalypse

This chapter offers only a brief overview of astrology. (For more detail, readers are advised to read a comprehensive book on astrology.) The attributes assigned to Sun signs, planets in the Zodiacs, planets in houses, and aspect patterns all were developed thousands of years ago by sages and scholars, based on collected data.

Principles of Astrology

The ecliptic is the path that the Sun forms during a year, as viewed from Earth. The celestial equator is Earth's equator, projected outward onto the celestial sphere. The ecliptic lies at an angle of 23.5° to the celestial equator (Figure 1.1). This means that the ecliptic and celestial equator cross each other at two points. These two points are called the vernal equinox and the autumnal equinox, otherwise known as the March equinox (the first point of the Sun sign Aries) and the September equinox (first point of the Sun sign Libra). The two points at which the ecliptic is farthest from the celestial equator are called the solstices. The summer solstice occurs in June, when the Sun enters Cancer, and winter solstice occurs in December, when the Sun enters Capricorn.

A constellation is a group of celestial bodies that are connected together in some arrangement. Constellations that lie within 7 to 8 degrees on either side of the ecliptic are called Zodiacs. Twelve Zodiacs divide the ecliptic into twelve equal parts, each of 30 degrees (Figure 1.2). Each month the Sun is in a different Zodiac of the ecliptic. The names of the twelve Zodiacs are as follows: Aries, Taurus, Gemini, Cancer, Leo, Virgo, Libra, Scorpio, Sagittarius, Capricorn, Aquarius, and Pisces.

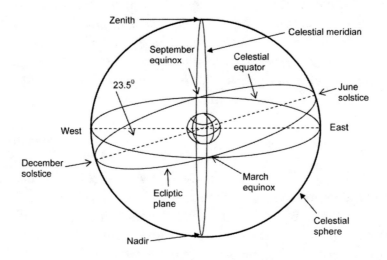

Figure 1.1: The ecliptic and celestial equator

Figure 1.1: The ecliptic and celestial equator

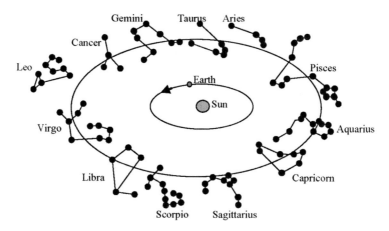

Figure 1.2: Zodiacs on the ecliptic

Figure 1.2: Zodiacs on the ecliptic

There are three principal elements of astrology:

1. Zodiacs

2. Planets

3. Horoscopes or natal charts

Each Zodiac sign is associated with one of the quadruplicities: cardinal, fixed, or mutable. Quadruplicity is a group of four Zodiacs. Cardinal people are action-oriented. Aries, Cancer, Libra, and Capricorn are cardinals. Fixed people are stable, preferring status quo. Taurus, Leo, Scorpio, and Aquarius are fixed. Mutable people are versatile and adaptable. Gemini, Virgo, Sagittarius, and Pisces are mutable.

Because astrology studies the influence of cosmic events on humans and earthly events, Earth is the center around which all the celestial bodies and planets rotate, according to the tenet of astrology. Therefore, in astrology, the Sun and Moon are considered as planets. The ten planets in Western astrology are as follows: Sun, Moon, Mercury, Venus, Mars, Jupiter, Saturn, Uranus, Neptune, and Pluto. Indian or Vedic astrology uses nine planets, which does not include Uranus, Neptune, and Pluto but consists of Sun (*Surya*), Moon

(*Chandra*), Mars (*Mangala*), Mercury (*Budha*), Jupiter (*Brihaspati*), Venus (*Shukra*), Saturn (*Shani*), North Lunar Node (*Rahu*), and South Lunar Node (*Ketu*). *Rahu* is a malefic force, and *Ketu* provides supernatural influence. The North Node is the point where the Moon climbs the ecliptic; the South Node is the point where the Moon sinks below the ecliptic.

Horoscope Chart

The horoscope chart is a wheel that shows the cosmic picture at a person's moment of birth. The wheel is divided into twelve equal houses, with each house occupying 30 degrees of the circle. Each house is associated with a different part of life. Figure 1.3 shows a natural wheel chart, with each Zodiac sign occupying a house. The name of the line in the chart that marks the beginning of the house is called the cusp. The cusp of the first house is 0 degrees and 0 minutes of Aries and is the beginning of the natural wheel. It corresponds to the spring equinox and is the natural start of four seasons. Reading the natural wheel counterclockwise, 30 degrees later is the second house cusp and is the beginning of Taurus. Following the cusps counterclockwise, the Zodiac signs follow sequentially. The natal horoscope chart or birth chart captures the positions of the planets in the Zodiac in the sky at one's birth time.

In order to create a birth chart, it is absolutely essential to learn about two things: the ephemeris (a good source is Alan Leo's Casting the Horoscope[1]) and the table of houses. The ephemeris is a table of values that shows where every planet was, is, and will be for every day, past, present, and future. The table of houses contains 360 charts, one for each degree of the horoscope wheel. Each chart contains the data necessary to calculate the degrees and signs on each house cusp for a given birth time and place.

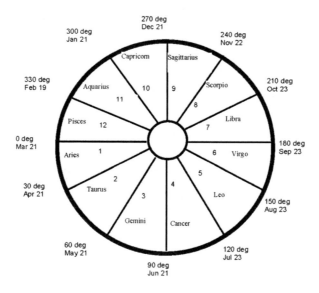

Figure 1.3: Horoscope chart

Figure 1.3: Horoscope chart

The astronomical clock, registering sidereal time, completes twenty-four hours during the time that Earth executes one complete rotation (i.e., it turns through 360 degrees). But in the twenty-four hours that it takes Earth to make one complete rotation, Earth has moved 1 degree backward, as it moves counterclockwise around the Sun. Hence, the Sun has moved 1 degree forward, relative to Earth. Consequently, Earth must turn 361 degrees, or thereabouts, before the Sun can be exactly on the meridian. This is a clock time of twenty-four hours, where Earth has actually turned 361 degrees. The sidereal time needs an additional 4 minutes to turn the extra 1 degree. Hence, 24 hours of clock time is equal to 24 hours 4 minutes of sidereal time. The ephemeris gives the sidereal time for each date of a year at Greenwich.

A time zone is a region of the Earth that has adopted the same standard time, usually referred to as the local time. Most adjacent time zones are exactly one hour apart, and by convention compute their local time as an offset from Greenwich mean time (GMT). Standard time zones can be defined by geometrically subdividing

Earth's spheroid into twenty-four wedge-shaped sections, bordered by meridians, each 15 degrees of longitude apart. The local time in neighboring zones would differ by one hour, but political and geographical practicalities can result in irregularly shaped zones that follow political boundaries or change their time seasonally, as with daylight saving time. For example, New York and Toronto follow eastern standard time (EST), which is the time at 75 degrees longitude west of Greenwich.

If a person is born in New York at 7 a.m., then it means 7 a.m. EST, relating to 75° west longitude. However, the longitude of New York is 73° 53' west. Each degree of longitude corresponds to 4 minutes of clock time. Each minute of longitude corresponds to 4 seconds of clock time. Because New York is situated at 1° 7' east of 75° longitude, the time difference is 4 minutes + (7 x 4) seconds = 4 minutes 28 seconds. Subtracting this time from a person's standard birth time, the true local time of the person's birth is 6 hours 55 minutes 32 seconds. In astrology, the true local time is important when casting a person's horoscope.

The process of casting a horoscope is as follows.

1. Calculate the true local clock time of birth by using the local standard clock time from the longitude of the birth place.

2. Determine the sidereal time at Greenwich that corresponds to the date of birth from the ephemeris.

3. Add correction for the sidereal time to the true local time, if the person was born in Greenwich.

4. Add correction for the sidereal time for birth places elsewhere (i.e., not in Greenwich).

5. Add the true local time from number 1 (above) and the corrections from numbers 3 and 4 (above) to the sidereal time at Greenwich from number 4. This gives the final calculated sidereal time.

6. Find the house cusps from the table of houses.

7. Calculate the planet positions from the ephemeris.

Sun Signs

A Sun sign represents the Zodiac that the Sun was in at the time of a person's birth. It can be determined quickly from the date of birth and Zodiac sign related to that date. There are twelve Sun signs representing twelve Zodiacs. The attributes and qualities of each Sun sign are given below.[2]

Aries: Arians are action-oriented and competitive and strive to be first in everything, often to the point of ignoring the rights of others. If they can learn to temper their aggressiveness with diplomacy, they can accomplish much. They are natural leaders, starting things for others to finish. They are dynamic, aggressive, impulsive, quarrelsome, easily bored, selfish, enthusiastic, and forceful.

Taurus: Taurus people are very stable and reliable, although quite stubborn. Their characteristics are materialism, greed, laziness, patience, steadiness, and endurance. They have inertia to begin, but always finish what they start. They are fiercely loyal to their friends. They are great planners and like comfort and possessions of all sorts.

Gemini: Geminis are the most intelligent people of all Zodiacs. They are quick-minded and are curious about virtually everything, but they lack self-discipline and the staying power to finish what they start. Thus, they can become jack-of-all-trades and master of none. If they acquire self-discipline, there is nothing they cannot achieve. They prefer multitasking, being involved in many pursuits at the same time. They are great communicators. They pursue intellectual activities such as philosophy, science, writing, and giving speech. They need to acquire calmness or they risk burning out their nervous system. They are witty, inquisitive, intelligent, versatile, but tend to be fickle and superficial. Their interests are learning, writing, reading, communication, travel, and knowing everything.

Cancer: Cancer people are the most sensitive, and home and family life are of utmost importance to them. They will do any thing to protect domestic security. They are very emotional and complex people and are easily hurt by others. They are difficult to understand; therefore, they do not get the necessary understanding from others. They are very loving, clinging to the people they love. They are shy and moody and can be cruel enemies. They are touchy, sentimental, tenacious, and react from intuition than from reason.

Leo: Leo people are noble and generous, with oversized egos. They are courageous, loyal, and like to be in charge, but they can be blunt, overconfident, and outspoken. They are strongly attracted to the opposite sex and are romantic, ambitious, temperamental, egotistical, generous, enthusiastic, optimistic, domineering, and affectionate.

Virgo: Virgo people are very thorough and detailed. They will do well in any line of work that requires precision and exactness. They are practical and efficient, but they are judgmental and very critical of others. They become so immersed in detail that they may lose sight of the big picture. They tend to worry a lot, which adversely affects their health. More Virgos remain unmarried than any other sign because of their high standards. They are methodical, neat, reliable, critical, industrious, and cautious.

Libra: Libra people have balanced judgment, making them good counselors or judges, clearly seeing both sides of an issue. This ability, however, sometimes can cause problems when making decisions in minor matters. They need companionship, and to them, marriage is important. They prefer an occupation that brings them in partnership with others. They work hard and possess a strong sense of justice and fair play. They rarely express anger, but when they do, it is a storm. They are romantic, dependenable, gracious, cooperative, and somewhat materialistic, and they do not hold grudges.

Scorpio: Scorpios have strong will power, with intense emotional and sexual drive. They do things with intensity and completeness, without fear of death. They are "workaholics," driving themselves hard and driving others unmercifully. They despise weakness in themselves and others. They are secretive and can become ruthless competitors and enemies. They are heroic, forceful, vindictive, determined, cynical, sarcastic, and suspicious.

Sagittarius: Sagittarians are honest and freedom-loving. No matter how difficult a situation becomes, there always seems to be help for them, because they are always under some sort of protective shield. They call the shots as they see them, making them blunt, lacking in tact. Women Sagittarians are charming but dislike domestic tasks, making them quite independent. They are optimistic, friendly, idealistic, and easy-going. They are interested in religion, philosophy, travel, and giving advice.

Capricorn: Capricorns are frugal, hardworking, and dedicated to achieving their goals. By maintaining integrity, they can achieve the highest of accomplishments. But without lack of integrity, they will have the greatest downfalls. They are undefeatable enemies and loyal friends. They are methodical and often are perceived as slave drivers. They need to be in charge, and do not function well in a subordinate position. They are ambitious, serious, realistic, cautious, and responsible.

Aquarius: Aquarians are loyal friends, tireless workers, and humanitarians. They have desire for material gain, but they are not greedy. They take work seriously, and do not demand more than their fair share. They have a great dislike for hypocrisy. They are determined, stubborn, and often argumentative. They are independent, broad-minded, dogmatic, rebellious, and tactless.

Pisces: Pisceans are the mixtures of all Zodiacs, hence their complex qualities. They are very sensitive people, responsive to the thoughts and feelings of others. They are often unable to make up their mind. They have a martyr complex and can be so combative that no one can reason with them. They alternate between optimism and pessimism. They are not ambitious people and turn into some dream world. They may be excellent artists, as they can have an overactive imagination. They are blind to any faults in the one they love. They are compassionate, psychic, day-dreamers, and changeable.

Ascendant or Rising Sign

The ascendant or rising sign is that Zodiac sign that is on the horizon (rising) at the person's moment of birth.

Triplicities

In astrology, a triplicity is a group of three Zodiacs, each associated with one of four elements: fire, earth, air, or water.

Fire: Aries, Leo, and Sagittarius; enthusiastic, energetic, and optimistic

Earth: Taurus, Virgo, and Capricorn; practical, down-to-earth, and realistic

Air: Gemini, Libra, and Aquarius; intellectual, communicative, thinker, and insensitive to others

Water: Cancer, Scorpio, and Pisces; emotional, sensitive, intuitive, and moody

Midheaven

The midheaven is abbreviated to MC, from the Latin *medium coeli*. Midheaven is the intersection of the celestial meridian with the ecliptic at birth. The celestial meridian is an imaginary great circle on the celestial sphere. It passes through the north point on the horizon, through the celestial pole, up to the zenith, through the south point on the horizon, and through the nadir, and is perpendicular to the local horizon (Figure 1.1). The significance of the midheaven is that it relates to the career of an individual and the way it is pursued. It also provides an indication of aims and intentions and the type of partner that may be sought. The point opposite to the midheaven is the *imum coeli*, or IC.

Aspect

The aspect is the relationship between two planets, expressed in degrees and minutes, at the birth moment. This relationship can be benefic or malefic, and it is very important for analysis. The aspects and their symbols are given in Table 1.1, but planets do not have the exact number of degrees. There is a plus/minus allowance, and this allowance is called *orb*.

Table 1.1: Aspects

Name of Aspect	Number of degrees apart	Orb degree
Conjunction	0	10
Sextile	60	4
Square	90	8
Trine	120	6
Opposition	180	10

Aspect Patterns

Aspect patterns are a particular combination of aspects that form special planetary configurations. There are a number of aspect patterns that involve three or more planets. The main aspect patterns are grand trine, grand cross, T-squares, and stellium.

Grand trine occurs when three planets form a triangle with trine aspects to each other, as shown in Figure 1.4a. Grand trines are positive and creative aspects, representing an opportunity granted, with an open and effortless flow of energy.

Grand trine fire has self-confidence, high aspiration, and emotion; it is outgoing and would benefit by conserving enthusiasm and impulsive nature.

Grand trine earth is action-oriented, with dependability and practicality.

Grand trine air is idealistic, turbo-charged, and adept at forming ideas; it has great mental faculties but is prone to depression.

Grand trine water has high creative potential and is instinctive and oversensitive.

Grand cross is made up of four planets in a four-cornered square that form four squares and two oppositions, as shown in Figure 1.4b. Grand cross is a very stressful and disruptive configuration. It offers a solid foundation, but to take advantage of it is very challenging. Because of the separation of four planets, each will fall in the same triplicities (i.e., cardinal, fixed, and mutable).

Cardinal grand cross implies a desire and will to overcome difficulties but a lack of self-confidence could be a barrier.

Fixed grand cross is stubborn and tolerates the status quo.

Mutable grand cross implies adaptability but may scatter and become disjointed under pressure.

T-square configuration consists of two planets in opposition with a third, which makes a square aspect to both the other planets, as shown in Figure 1.4c. All the aspects so constructed are negative, but it often confers strength, mostly depending on the planet that receives the two squares. It causes lot of difficulties in life, but they also spark action and a drive to achieve success. T-square is an impetus to success for many famous people.

Cardinal T-square has exceptional dynamism and energy.

Fixed T-square is exceptionally stubborn, fighting personal causes and ideas to the end.

Mutable T-square solves problems by being flexible and adaptable.

Stellium consists of a group of three or more planets forming conjunctions to one another, within an orb of 10 degrees or less in the same house. The tighter the orb, the stronger the effect of the stellium. Individual planets strengthen the particular zodiac containing the stellium. The stellium is a mega-planet devoting mega-energy in the activity revealed by the Zodiac and house of the stellium.

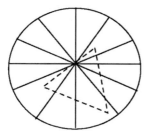

Figure 1.4A: Grand Trine   **Figure 1.4B:** Grand Cross

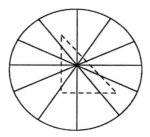

Figure 1.4C: T-Square

Houses

There are three types of houses: angular, succedent, and cadent.

Angular houses are the first, fourth, seventh, and tenth houses. Planets placed in these houses have a greater scope of action than the planets placed in other houses. When the majority of planets are in angular houses, it means the person will have a prominent position in the world.

Succedent houses are the second, fifth, eighth, and eleventh houses. Planets placed in these houses tend to give stability, will power, and purpose but no great activity. When the majority of the planets are in the succedent houses, it indicates that the person may be stubborn and uncompromising.

Cadent houses are the third, sixth, ninth, and twelfth houses. Planets placed in these houses generally show very little activity. When the majority of the planets are in cadent houses, the person likely has very little public recognition.

Each house is ruled by a planet. The ruling planets and attributes[2] of the houses are shown in Table 1.2.

Table 1.2: Ruling Planets and Attributes of Houses

House	Type	Ruling Planet	Strength	Attributes
First	Angular	Mars	High	Physical body and personality, self-awareness, self-interest
Second	Succedent	Venus	Medium	Income, money, possessions, material resource
Third	Cadent	Mercury	Low	Communication, thought process, mental activity, relatives, travel
Fourth	Angular	Moon	High	Domestic life, home
Fifth	Succedent	Sun	Medium	Romance, children, creative ability, entertainment
Sixth	Cadent	Mercury	Low	Health, working condition, service to others, love for animals
Seventh	Angular	Venus	High	Marriage, partnership, relations with others
Eighth	Succedent	Pluto	Medium	Death, inheritance, insurance, taxes, investigation
Ninth	Cadent	Jupiter	Low	Religion, foreign travel, publishing, education, legal matters
Tenth	Angular	Saturn	High	Profession, ambition, reputation, honors, social and professional status
Eleventh	Succedent	Uranus	Medium	Friends, relations, hopes, dreams
Twelfth	Cadent	Neptune	Low	Secrets, enemies, delusion, psychic matters, work behind scene

Each Zodiac is ruled by one planet,[3] as shown in Table 1.3.

Table 1.3: Ruling Planets of Zodiacs

Zodiac	Ruling planet	Zodiac	Ruling planet
Aries	Mars	Libra	Venus
Taurus	Venus	Scorpio	Mars
Gemini	Mercury	Sagittarius	Jupiter
Cancer	Moon	Capricorn	Saturn
Leo	Sun	Aquarius	Uranus
Virgo	Mercury	Pisces	Neptune

Each planet placed in each Zodiac has different attributes. The attributes of the planets in Zodiacs are given in Appendix 1[4]; similarly, the attributes of the planets placed in different houses are given in Appendix 2[4].

This gives in a nutshell the techniques used in astrology to determine the character, strengths, and weaknesses of a person.

> *There is no better boat than a horoscope to help a man cross over the sea of life.*

—Varaha Mihira (Indian astronomer)

Chapter 2
History of Astrology

Perhaps there is a pattern set up in the universe for the one who desires to see it, and having seen it, to find one in himself.

—Plato

Astrology is an ancient science that started five thousand to six thousand years ago when Babylonian priests made maps of the skies. The oldest astrological text is found in the Babylonian period around 1830 BCE. Regular occurrences of months, seasons, and years were important to the Babylonians. Their interest was the well-being of the country and the king, not of individuals. Their predictions mainly involved the weather, harvests, drought, storm, famine, war, and fates of kings. Hence, astrology at that time was omen astrology.

Around the world, farmers plant most crops in the spring and harvest in the fall. But in some regions, there is not much differentiation between the seasons. Because different constellations are visible at different times of the year, one can use the constellations to tell which month it is. For example, Scorpius is only visible in the Northern Hemisphere's evening sky in the summer. Some historians suspect that many of the myths associated with the constellations were invented to help the farmers remember the constellations. When they saw certain constellations, they would know it was time to begin the planting or reaping. In course of time, this dependence on the sky became a strong part of many cultures. Many nomadic tribes followed the night skies when moving from one location to another.

With the Assyrians, omen astrology became profoundly important. The priest-astronomer-astrologer presented to the king's court at regular intervals his predictions for the Assyrian state, and his words were regarded with reverence and respect. In the absence of any calendar as a guide for the seasons, and due to the burden of responsibility entrusted to them, the priests observed the bright stars and star patterns at night during each month, as an indicator for each month. The earliest star maps were found around 1000 BCE. The twelve Zodiac constellations were finalized around 600 BCE. The signs of the Zodiacs were completed in late 400s BCE.

The calendars in Mesopotamia were lunar. Months were measured by noting one complete orbit of the Moon around Earth with the appearance of the first crescent Moon after sunset. In order to correlate one solar year with lunar years, it was necessary every few years to introduce a thirteenth month in the calendar. Egyptians introduced later solar years by associating the annual flooding of the Nile River with the rising star Sirius.

The oldest known horoscope is Babylonian, from around 410 BCE. With the introduction of astrology and astronomy into Greece around 400 BCE, astrology and horoscopes developed considerably. As the Greek culture was introduced into Egypt, both astronomy and astrology were actively cultivated in the region of the Nile during the Hellenistic and Roman periods. It is believed that the Babylonians instructed the priests of the pharaohs in astrology, and monuments still exist in Egypt indicating that the Egyptians during the Hellenistic period had working knowledge of astrology.

Noted Practitioners of Astrology

Greek philosopher Thales (c. 643–c.546 BCE) studied astronomy and astrology. So did Greek philosopher and mathematician Pythagoras (c.569–c.475 BCE). Greek philosopher Plato (c.428–c.348 BCE) studied and practiced astrology. Greek physician Hippocrates (c.460–c.370 BCE), who is called the "father of medicine," combined astrology with medical diagnosis. Greek mathematician, astronomer, and astrologer Claudius Ptolemaeus (CE 100–178), known in English as Ptolemy, wrote the *Tetrabiblos*, the earliest surviving book on astrology. *Tetrabiblos* was the most popular astrological work in antiquity and also enjoyed great influence in the Islamic world and the medieval Latin West. The *Tetrabiblos* is an extensive and continually reprinted treatise on the ancient principles of horoscopic astrology, written in four books. It is strongly believed that Galileo was involved with astrology. The letters by Galileo to his astrological colleagues have been lost; only the replies remain. Likewise the most famous charts composed by him have been lost, but some twenty-five charts drawn up by him do still remain, plus several instances of his chart analyses.

In Rome and the Roman empire, astrology was widely practiced, and great faith was placed in the work and advice of the astrologers who were appointed by the emperors. The Moon was considered particularly influential and was depicted on many of their coins. Greek neoplatonic philosopher Porphyry (CE c.232–c.309) wrote widely on astrology and is said to have developed the house method in astrology. Julius Maternus was a Roman writer and astrologer who wrote *Matheseos Libri Octo* (*Eight Books of Astrology*, c. 330.)

Astrology was further developed by the Arabs from the seventh to the thirteenth centuries. By the early thirteenth century, interest in astrology was rekindled in Europe. Astrologers were dominating influences at courts in Europe. Astrology was divided into three distinct fields: natural or mundane astrology, which involved forecasting national events, weather, etc.; horary astrology, which deals with answering question by studying the astrological charts set for the exact time and place of asking the question; and judicial astrology, which determines the fortune of an individual by using the birth chart.

In India and China, astrology developed largely independently. Indian astrology is Vedic in origin and has been part of Hindu teachings, dating back four thousand years. Chinese astrology, as called by Westerners, is not only Chinese—it has a long history in other East Asian countries, such as Japan, Thailand, and Vietnam. Astrology is believed to have originated in China at the time of Shang dynasty (c. 1766 BCE–1050 BCE).

During this period, astrology and astronomy went hand in hand. There was no bitter distinction between them, as it is today. Medical practices also were entwined with astrology. Astrology was taught at academic centers along with philosophy, arts, music, architecture, and politics. There was little antagonism between astrology and the Church at that time; in fact, astrology was practiced by the Church.

Swiss alchemist and physician Phillipus Paracelsus (1493–1541) was also an astrologer. He believed that the Sun, planets, and stars influenced people for good or evil. French seer Michel de Nostredame, better known as Nostradamus, who published collections of prophecies in the famous book *Les Propheties*, was a practicing astrologer. The nobility and other prominent persons from faraway places would ask Nostradamus for horoscopes and advice. Nostradamus claimed to base his astrology on judicial astrology, which is the art of forecasting future events by calculation of the planetary and stellar bodies and their relationship to Earth. The term judicial astrology was mainly used in the Middle Ages and early Renaissance to distinguish between the natural astrology, such as medical astrology and meteorological astrology, which were seen as acceptable because they were a part of the natural sciences of the time. Today, this distinction is largely obsolete.

Through history, many famous and celebrated figures either practiced astrology or employed their own astrologers. I will mention here some of the well-documented cases. During the sixteenth century, Queen Elizabeth 1 of England commissioned astrologer and scientist John Dee to determine the most auspicious date for her coronation. During the English civil war, between 1642 and 1651, astrologers worked with the armed forces of both sides. One of the astrologers, William Lilly, later predicted, in 1652, the Great Fire of London so accurately that he was summoned to appear before a committee investigating the causes of the fire. There was a suspicion that the fire had been started deliberately, and Lilly's enemies tried to implicate him.

Alexander the Great was known to have consulted with astrologers regularly. An image of Alexander the Great consulting his astrologers with regard to an eclipse of the Sun after the battle of Arbela can be found in the British Library. William Shakespeare used astrological events, forecasts, and metaphors extensively in his plays and poetry. Shakespeare was very knowledgeable about astrology and held its practice in high regard, which can be seen in examples from his plays. In the play *All's Well That Ends Well*, the heroine of the play, Helena, obviously understands astrological concepts and uses them to her advantage. In her dialogue with Parolles, a retainer of her intended husband, she refers to him as being "born under a charitable star." When he replies that he was born when Mars was predominant, she retorts, "When he was retrograde, I think, rather." By retrograde, Helena refers to the phenomenon of the apparent backward motion of Mars as seen from Earth, which occurs approximately every two years. A retrograde Mars could signify someone who is deceptive, cowardly, and unable to take direct action when called upon. In the tragedy *King Lear,* astrology is used to a great effect. Gloucester, one of the more sympathetic characters in the play, equates the troubles in the land to the recent eclipses. Eclipses are one of the most powerful events in astrology, portending great upheaval in the places where they can be seen.

There is a popular and apocryphal anecdote about Isaac Newton with regard to astrology. When the British astronomer Edmund Halley (discoverer of Halley's Comet) supposedly spoke deprecatingly about astrology to Newton, Newton is said to have responded, "I have studied the matter [astrology]; you, sir, have not." This shows Newton's interest in astrology.

Sydney Omarr, a prominent astrologer whose column appeared in more than three hundred newspapers across the country, including the *Washington Post*, made a startling revelation in 1988 about the Reagan administration. President Reagan and First Lady Nancy regularly consulted the astrologers to guide in the making of important decisions in the White House. As for Ronald Reagan, like Calvin Coolidge, Theodore Roosevelt, and Franklin D. Roosevelt before him, astrology appeared to be tied into life itself, and important decisions required at least a quick glance to the stars. The *Philadelphia Inquirer*, for example, insisted that "the signing of the U.S.–Soviet treaty eliminating medium-range nuclear missiles" had been signed at 1:30 p.m. on December 8, 1987, based on the advice from an astrologer. In addition, many newspapers reported the story that Ronald Reagan had postponed by nine minutes his inauguration as the governor of California on January 2, 1967, based on astrology calculations.

Reagan became noted as one of the few governors to actually sign astrology-related legislation. On August 30, 1974, he signed legislation that removed licensed astrologers in Sacramento from the category of fortune tellers, thus allowing them to practice their trade for compensation. In one interview published in the *Wall Street Journal*, Sydney Omarr made a stunning revelation: that the Reagans were not the only high-level Washingtonians to have looked to the stars. Omarr told the *Wall Street Journal*, that former President Richard Nixon and Henry Kissinger also were "gung-ho" on astrology.

Using astrology to predict money markets and the economy has a long and repeated history. A recent article in the *British Astrological Journal* discovered that approx 40% of Wall Street stockbrokerage firms use astrology. Daniel Pallant, an investment analyst who occasionally writes for the *Financial Press*, specializes in astrological financial forecast. Sam Crawford, who uses a combination of technical analysis and planetary cycles to predict the direction of financial markets, has published a monthly newsletter since 1977 and maintains a phone hotline for stock tips. In addition to being an astrologer, Crawford is a skilled technical analyst. Online research indicates that Crawford successfully predicted market downturns in 1987, as well as the 2000 bear market and the financial crash that occurred after 9/11. Last February, he successfully predicted the prewar downturn and was featured in *Forbes* as the only astrologer to be tracked by the respected *Hubert Financial Digest*.

British astrologer John Addey developed the harmonic approach to astrology, which means that every link between every pair of planets in a horoscope has some significance. He isolated some interesting features regarding illnesses, such as polio. Although his work was not subjected to rigorous statistical analysis, the results are encouraging.

Astrology and Astronomy Branching out

In the beginning, astrology was intimately combined with astronomy. The split between them essentially began when Copernicus (1473–1543), a Prussian astronomer, formulated a heliocentric model of the solar system, where the Sun, instead of Earth, is at the center, with the planets orbiting around it. Copernicus explained the backward motion of Mars as being due to Earth overtaking Mars, since Earth's orbital period (one year) is shorter than Mars'.

The greatest champions of the Copernican system were Johannes Kepler (1571–1630), German astronomer and mathematician, and Galileo Galilei (1564–1642), Italian astronomer and physicist. Kepler discovered that Earth—as well as the planets that travel around Sun—travel in elliptical orbits. He formulated three fundamental laws of planetary motion, which can be described as follows:

- The law of ellipses: the paths of the planets around the Sun are elliptical in shape, with the center of the Sun being located at one focus.

- The law of equal areas: an imaginary line drawn from the center of the Sun to the center of the planet will sweep out equal areas in equal intervals of time.

- The law of harmonies: the ratio of the squares of the periods of any two planets is equal to the ratio of the cubes of their average distances from the Sun.

Galileo has been called the "father of modern observational astronomy," and his contributions covered a wide area. Best known are the discoveries he made using telescopes. He discovered the four biggest moons of Jupiter and the existence of sunspots. However, Galileo's heliocentric model of the solar system was condemned by the Catholic Church as contrary to scripture, and he spent the last years of life under house arrest on orders of the Inquisition.

From early times it was found that while most stars remained fixed, five, in particular, did not; they wandered about the sky. These actually were the planets Mercury, Venus, Mars, Jupiter, and Saturn.

The discovery of three other planets—Uranus, Neptune, and Pluto—followed the invention of the telescope. Uranus was discovered by William Herschel in 1781; John Adams and Urbain Le Verrier discovered Neptune in 1846; and Clyde Tombaugh discovered Pluto in 1930. Originally classified as a planet in astronomy, Pluto has been reclassified as a dwarf planet orbiting the Sun.

Solar System

The solar system consists of the Sun and the other celestial objects gravitationally bound to it: the eight planets, their 165 known moons, three dwarf planets (Ceres, Pluto, and Eris and their four known moons), and billions of small bodies, including asteroids, Kuiper Belt objects, comets, meteoroids, and interplanetary dust.

Mercury, Venus, Earth, and Mars are called are called inner planets. The inner planets have a compact, rocky surface. Jupiter, Saturn, Uranus, Neptune, and Pluto are called outer planets; these are all gaseous.

An asteroid belt composed of rocky bodies lies between the inner planets and the outer planets. A second belt, the Kuiper Belt, is composed of icy objects and lies beyond the outer planets. Ceres, one of the dwarf planets, is the largest object in the asteroid belt; Eris lies outside the Kuiper belt.

The orbits of the planets are ellipses, with the Sun at one focus of the ellipse. The orbits of the planets are more or less in the same plane, called the ecliptic plane, which is the geometric plane that contains the mean orbit of Earth around the Sun. Only Pluto's orbit lies about 17.5° out of the ecliptic plane.

The Sun is a sphere of extremely hot incandescent gas, with a diameter of 864,000 miles at an average distance of 93 million miles from Earth. So large is its diameter that 109 Earths, stretched out like beads on a string, could be needed to cross it from side to side. Its enormous size could contain a million Earth-sized globules. The Sun accounts for 99.8% of the solar system's mass.

The Sun consists of hydrogen (about 74% of its mass, or 92% of its volume) and helium (about 25% of its mass, or 7% of its volume). The remaining 1% is made up of trace quantities of heavier elements, such as sodium, magnesium, iron, and calcium, and smaller quantities of sixty other substances, all in gaseous form. Although the Sun is composed of gas, its average density is 1.41 times that of Earth.

The Sun has a surface temperature of approximately 5,780 K (kelvin), giving it a white color. But because of atmospheric scattering, the Sun appears yellow, as seen from the surface of Earth. This is a subtractive effect, as the preferential scattering of blue photons (causing the blue sky color) removes enough blue light to leave a residual reddishness that is perceived as yellow. When low enough in the sky, the Sun appears orange or red due to this scattering.

Earth is the third planet from the Sun and is the only known planet in the universe to harbor life. Earth orbits the Sun at an average distance of 93 million miles every 365.2 solar days (one sidereal year). The sidereal year is the time taken for the Sun to return to the same position with respect to the stars of the celestial sphere. Earth's orbit around the Sun is slightly elliptical, with the distance from the Sun varying between 95.5 million and 91.9 million miles. Earth moves counterclockwise in its orbit around the Sun.

Earth's shape is very close to an oblate spheroid—a rounded shape with a bulge around the equator. The average diameter of the spheroid is about 7960 miles, so that the equatorial diameter is twenty-seven miles larger than the pole-to-pole diameter. Earth rotates counterclockwise around its axis once a day. Earth's axis is tilted at an angle of 23.5° to the ecliptic plane.

Earth's atmosphere is 78 percent nitrogen and 21 percent oxygen, with trace amounts of water vapor, carbon dioxide, and other gaseous molecules. Earth's atmosphere has no definite boundary; it slowly becomes thinner, fading into outer space. Three-quarters of the atmosphere's mass is contained within the first four miles of the planet's surface. This lowest layer is called the troposphere. Energy from the Sun heats this layer and the surface below, causing expansion of the air. This lower-density air then rises and is replaced by cooler higher-density air. The result is atmospheric circulation that drives the weather and climate through redistribution of heat energy.

Above the troposphere, the atmosphere is divided into the following: stratosphere, mesospohere, thermosphere, ionosphere, and exosphere. The stratosphere extends from the troposphere's 4 to 11 mile range to about 31 miles. Temperature increases with height. The stratosphere contains the ozone layer, the part of Earth's atmosphere that contains relatively high concentrations of ozone. The ozone layer is mostly responsible for absorbing ultraviolet radiation. The stratosphere is separated from mesosphere, the next layer above it, by stratopause. The mesosphere extends from about 31 miles to the range of 50 to 52 miles, temperature decreasing with height. The thermosphere extends from 50 to 52 miles to more than 400 miles, temperature increasing with height. The ionosphere is the part of the thermosphere that is ionized by solar radiation. It plays an important part in atmospheric electricity and forms the inner edge of the magnetosphere. It has practical importance because among other functions, it influences radio propagation to distant places on Earth. It is located in the thermosphere and is responsible for auroras. The exosphere extends from 400 to 600 miles up to 6000 miles and has free-moving particles that may migrate into and out of the magnetosphere or the solar wind.

Earth has only one Moon, which is Earth's nearest neighbor in space. The Moon is the only celestial body to which humans have traveled and upon which humans have landed. The average center-to-center distance from Earth to the Moon is 238,840 miles, which is about thirty times the diameter of Earth. The Moon has a diameter of 2,158 miles, slightly more than a quarter of the diameter of Earth and a little smaller than the length across the United States. The Moon makes a complete orbit around Earth every 27.3 days.

The orbital period and rotational period of the Moon are the same—27.3 days. That is why the Moon keeps nearly the same face turned towards Earth at all times. The Moon orbits Earth in a counterclockwise direction, the same direction as Earth rotates. The Moon appears to shine by reflecting sunlight. A solar eclipse occurs when the Moon's shadow crosses Earth's surface, and a lunar eclipse occurs when the Moon moves into the shadow of Earth.

Mercury is the solar system's smallest planet and nearest to the Sun. It has a diameter of 3000 miles and an orbital revolution period of 88 Earth days (its year) and an axial rotation period of 59 Earth days (its days). Mercury has a mean distance of 36 million miles from the Sun. Surface temperature of Mercury ranges from about 90 to 700K (-180 to 430^{0}C). Mercury has a gravity of 0.38g, where g is the gravity of Earth. Its gravity is too small to retain any significant atmosphere over long periods of time.

Venus is the second closest planet to the Sun. It is the brightest natural object in the night sky, except for the Moon. Venus reaches its maximum brightness shortly before sunrise or shortly after sunset—this is why it is often called the morning star or the evening star. The distance of Venus from the Sun is 67 million miles, and its orbit is closer to being circular than any other planet. The orbital revolution period is 225 Earth days (its year), and its axial rotation period is 243 Earth days (its day). The diameter of Venus is 7,700 miles, which is 406 miles less than the Earth's diameter. Its mass is 81% of Earth's with a gravity of 0.9g. The enormously CO_2-rich atmosphere, along with thick clouds of sulfur dioxide, generates the strongest greenhouse effect in the solar system creating surface temperature over 460^{0}C.

Mars is the fourth planet from the Sun in the solar system. The planet is named after Mars, the Roman god of war. It is also referred to as the "Red Planet" because of its reddish appearance as seen from Earth. Mars has two moons, Phobos and Deimos, which are small and irregularly shaped. Mars has an average distance of 142 million miles from the Sun. It orbits the Sun once every 687 Earth days. Mars has a diameter of 4219 miles, nearly half of Earth's diameter. The mass of Mars 0.11 of Earth's and its gravity is 0.45g. The period of rotation about its axis is 24hr 37min, similar to Earth's. The atmosphere is quite dusty. Martian temperature varies from -140^{0}C during polar winters to 20^{0}C in summer. Current evidence suggests that Mars was once significantly more habitable than it is today. But whether living organisms ever existed is still unclear.

Jupiter is the fifth planet from the Sun and the largest planet, with a diameter of 89,000 miles. It is two and a half times as massive as all of the other planets in our solar system combined. Jupiter, along with Saturn, Uranus, and Neptune, is classified as a gas giant. Jupiter is named after the Roman god Jupiter. It orbits the Sun at every 11.86 years at an average distance of 484 million miles. Jupiter rotates once about its axis in 9 hr 51 min. Although this planet dwarfs Earth (with a diameter 11 times as great), it is considerably less dense. A volume equal to 1,317 Earths only contains 318 times as much mass. The temperature in the atmosphere is between -120⁰C to -170⁰C. Jupiter has at least 63 moons, the four largest of which are Lo, Europa, Ganymede, and Callisto.

Saturn is the sixth planet from the Sun and the second largest planet in the solar system. It was named after the Roman god Saturnus. Saturn orbits the Sun at a mean distance of 886 million miles, once every 29.46 Earth years. This is the only planet of the solar system that is less dense than water. Saturn is probably best known for its system of planetary rings, which makes it the most visually remarkable object in the solar system. The rings are split into a number of different parts, which include the bright A and B rings and a fainter C rings. Saturn has a large number of moons—as of 2007, a total of sixty individual moons have been identified, though many are very small. Only seven of them are massive enough with Titan as the most massive with 1.5 times the mass of Earth. The other three Saturn's moons in order of mass are Rhea, Lapetus, and Dione.

Uranus is the seventh planet from the Sun, is the third largest and fourth most massive planet in the solar system. It is named after the ancient Greek deity of the sky, Uranus. The planet is 1,784 million miles from the Sun, and its orbital revolution period is 84 Earth years. Uranus has the least mass of the giant planets. Its average diameter is 31,585 miles; its axial rotation period is 10 hrs 48 mins with an axial tilt of 98 degrees. Uranus' mass is roughly 14.5 times that of the Earth, making it the least massive of the giant planets. Uranus has a surface temperature of -200⁰C. Uranus has 27 known natural moons. The five main satellites are Miranda, Ariel, Umbriel, Titania, and Oberon. The largest of the satellites, Titania, has a radius of only 788.9 km, or less than half the radius of the Earth's Moon.

Neptune is the eighth and farthest known planet from the Sun in the solar system. The planet is named after the Roman god of the sea, Neptune. Its distance from Sun is 2,793 million miles, with an orbital revolution period of 165 years. Its diameter is 31,000 miles with an axial rotation period of 14 hrs and an axial tilt of 28.3 degrees. Neptune is 17 times the mass of Earth , and its surface temperature is -220⁰C. Neptune has 13 known moons. The largest by far, and the only one massive enough to be spheroidal, is Triton.

Pluto is named after god of underworld, Pluto, and has a mean distance of 3,666 million miles from the Sun. Pluto's orbit is highly eccentric with its orbit inclined about 17^0 to the ecliptic with a mean distance of 3,666 million miles from the Sun. It has an orbital revolution period of 248 Earth years, a diameter of 1470 miles, and rotates about its axis once every 6 Earth days. It has a surface temperature around -230⁰C. Because of low gravity and low temperature, it has no atmosphere. It has a small moon called Charon.

The asteroid belt is the region of the solar system located roughly between the orbits of Mars and Jupiter. It consists of asteroids that are small celestial bodies, composed of rock, ice, and some metal, that orbit the Sun. The asteroid belt has the dwarf planet, Ceres, which is about 590 miles in diameter.

The Kuiper Belt is a region of the solar system beyond the planets and extending from the orbit of Neptune (2793 million miles) to approximately 5120 million miles from the Sun. It is similar to the asteroid belt, although it is far larger—twenty times as wide and twenty to two hundred times as massive. Like the asteroid belt, it consists mainly of small bodies (remnants from the solar system's formation) and the dwarf planet Pluto. While the asteroid belt is composed primarily of rock, ice, and metal, the Kuiper Belt objects are composed largely of frozen volatiles (dubbed "ices"), such as methane, ammonia, and water.

Concluding Remarks

As astronomy broke away from astrology, astronomy became involved with the study of celestial objects (stars, planets, comets, and galaxies). Its current study is the evolution, physics, chemistry, meteorology, and motion of the celestial objects, as well the formation and development of the universe. As the scientists started researching the origin of the universe, this particular area branched out into a specialized area called cosmology, derived from the Greek word *cosmology*, which is the combination of *cosmos* (order) and *logos* (study). Cosmology involves physics and astrophysics by bringing observations and mathematical tools to analyze the universe as a whole—in other words, in the understanding of the universe through scientific observation and experiment.

Astrology, on the other hand, remained with its initial goal of studying the effect of planets and celestial objects on human life. Astrology's main principle is that the course of human life is related to the environment of the planets and celestial objects. This is aptly suggested by the ancient hermetic maxim:

As above, so below; as below, so above.

Chapter 3
Astrology is Based on
Statistical Analysis

There is an increasingly solid statistical link between
the time of birth of great men and their occupational
success. ... Having collected over 20,000 dates of birth of
professional celebrities from various European countries
and from the United States, I had to draw the unavoidable
conclusion that the position of the planets at birth is linked
to one's destiny. What a challenge to the rational mind.

—Michel Gauquelin, *Neo-Astrology,* 1991

In this chapter, I will describe the first "good" reason why astrology
is science: astrology is based on statistical analysis. As previously
mentioned, astrology was developed by collecting data of the
positions of the stars and planets in the sky and relating those data
to human life and events on Earth. Statistical analysis was a key tool
in this development and assigning of attributes to Sun signs, planets,
and houses. What follows are the basics of statistical analysis and
how it has been applied to astrology.

Statistical Analysis

Statistical analysis is the technique used to interpret collections of quantitative or numerical data. We can measure or count things, such as characteristics, traits, and features involving groups or objects, although they may apply also to repeated measurements of an individual or object. There are three categories of statistics[5]: descriptive statistics, sampling statistics, and predictive statistics. Descriptive statistics deals with large numbers, shows their distribution in value, and indicates how they tend to be alike or different in value. In sampling statistics, small groups of individuals (samples) are selected from larger groups, analyzed, and inferences are drawn about the larger groups (populations) from the results of the analysis of the samples.

In predictive astrology, suppose we know the relationship between a measure X and a measure Y from the analysis of groups of individuals. Now we are confronted with a new group of individuals for which only X measure is available. We are required to make some prediction of measure Y of this new group. We can make the prediction by using the new value of X, combined with the knowledge of the relationship between X and Y, based on our previous experience.

Let us consider, for example, a collection of incomes for a particular group of one thousand individuals, as shown in Table 3.1.

Table 3.1: Distribution of 1000 individual incomes

Annual income	Frequency	Interval size
150,000–200,000	5	50,000
125,000–149,999	20	25,000
100,000–124,999	50	25,000
80,000–99,999	120	20,000
70,000–79,999	180	10,000
60,000–69,999	220	10,000
50,000–59,999	280	10,000
40,000–49,999	75	10,000
30,000–39,999	40	10,000
20,000–29,999	7	10,000
10,000–19,999	2	10,000
0–9,999	1	10,000

The word frequency is used in this case to show the number in each interval. A frequency distribution is defined as a technique for presenting a collection of data in such a way as to show the number in each interval. From the income distribution in Table 4.4, the following conclusions can be derived:

80% of income lies between 50,000–100,000

0.075% of income lies above 100,000

0.125% of income lies below 50,000

The larger the number of samples, the more accurate will be the result of the analysis. Also, the study could be done over a large geographic area. However, for a large population, it becomes impossible to gather data from each individual. In that case, sampling techniques are used. A sample of individuals is selected from a large population and data relevant to the study is collected from the individuals. These sampled data are then analyzed to make the conclusion for the study with a certain error, called sampling error. More of this can be obtained from a standard book of statistics.[5]

Now, let us consider an example of how statistical analysis can be used in astrology. As noted in chapter two, attributes are assigned to each Sun sign. Let us consider a group of one thousand individuals with the Sun sign Aries, and collect data related to their characteristics, as shown in Table 3.2.

Table 3.2: Characteristics of Aries people

Characteristics	Frequency
Competitiveness	700
Aggressiveness	600
Leadership	500
Dynamism	500
Diplomacy	300
Reliability	250
Quarrelsome	300
Judgment	400
Family life	400
Social life	350

Data are shown just as an example.

From the analysis of the frequency of the characteristics, the following conclusions can be derived:

Aries people are competitive, aggressive, and dynamic and can achieve a lot if they are more diplomatic and use judgment. Their competitive drive may affect their family and social life.

Aries people are born between March 21 and April 21. In order to make the analysis more rigorous, a random sample of people born at different months of the year could be taken and data related to the characteristics in Table 3.2 could be collected and analyzed. The same study could be performed for other Sun signs. Thousands of years ago, ancient sages and scholars would not have used the current sophisticated statistical analysis techniques when analyzing people's birth times and characteristics. That is why I strongly believe that an intensive statistical analysis study should be taken to place astrology on a firmer scientific basis.

Statistical Analysis by Gauquelin

French psychologist and statistician Michel Gauquelin[6] (1928–1991), along with his first wife, Françoise Schneider-Gauquelin, conducted very important statistical research on astrology. Gauquelin showed an interest in astrology from an early age; it is said that he could calculate a birth chart at the age of ten and earned the nickname "Nostradamus" at school because of his astrology readings. After studying psychology and statistics at the Sorbonne university, he devoted his life to demonstrating the validity of certain fundamentals of astrology. However, he did not define himself as an astrologer; in fact, he opposed the practice of astrology, although his father was an enthusiastic defender of astrology.

Over the years, Gauquelin[7] studied many thousands of birth charts and submitted them to rigorous statistical analysis. He analyzed the charts to establish a correlation between the positions of the planets, the day of an individual's birth, the person's psychological character, and the effect of this character on destiny. His line of research explored astrology scientifically, not as an attempt to empirically prove the astrology handed down by tradition but rather to test astrology reformulated by science. He found a high frequency of placements of certain planets in the birth charts of eminent professionals, such as athletes, doctors, actors, etc.

Most notably, Gauquelin discovered the "Mars effect," which was derived from a study and analysis of more than two thousand eminent athletes' birth charts. He found that there were a significantly higher number of these athletes—higher than chance would allow—who had Mars either around the ascendant (ASC) or the midheaven (MC), as shown in Figure 3.1. The diagram in Figure 3.1 is basically a graph turned into a circle. The larger and larger circles emanating from the center indicate the frequency or number of the hits, while the circle itself represents the 360 degrees of the horoscope chart. The dotted line shows the frequency, or number, of planet Mars, placed in different houses of the planets, with peaks near ASC and MC. In astrological terms, a planet is said to be strong when it is rising corresponding to the ASC or culminating corresponding to the MC. The same is true for other planets and other professions:

Jupiter for eminent politicians and executives; Saturn for scientists and physicians; and the Moon for successful writers. This seems to be in line with astrology, which always associates Mars with competitive spirit, Jupiter with politics, Saturn with concentration, and the Moon with imagination.

Gauquelin also revealed relationships between the natal charts of parents and children. He found that where a parent has a planet on a certain angle in his or her birth chart, the child will also have the same planet on the same angle. This applies to natural births only. When births are forced or manipulated, the effect disappears. This discovery of natural hereditary/planetary link is another of Gauquelin's important works.

Gauquelin tried to reform astrology by suggesting that astrologers should cast aside the majority of their tradition and build a new astrology based on the foundation, which can be proved statistically accurate and verifiable. He termed this as "neo-astrology," which is also the name of his final book. Gauquelin's work is often cited by astrologers as an evidence in favor of astrology.

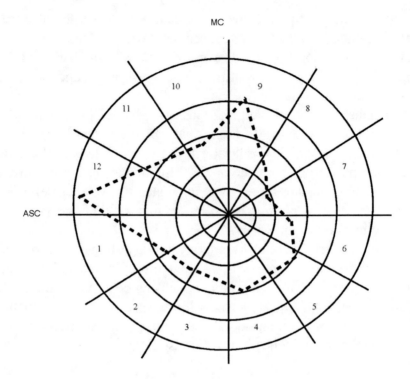

Figure 3.1: Gaquelin's Mars effect

Figure 3.1: Gauquelin's Mars effect

Gauquelin's statistical observations and results created a lively polemic within the scientific community. In 1960, the Belgian Committee for the Scientific Investigation of Claims of Paranormal Phenomenon (PARA) verified his assumptions and calculations. There was perfect agreement, as emphasized by the Belgian Committee PARA, between Gauquelin and the group of scientists with regard to the establishment of an experimental protocol, as well as to the calculation of standards and statistical formulas for the sampling. The committee arrived at the same findings for the positions of Mars in the first and ninth houses, which seemed abnormally elevated statistically. Nevertheless, the committee rejected Gauquelin's interpretation of the results, noting that Gauquelin didn't sufficiently confirm the calculations of the theoretical distribution of Mars, along with his disagreement of the committee's objections.

Support of Gauquelin's Work

Gauquelin's work found strong support from some influential scientists. Professor Hans Eysenck (1916–1997) was arguably the most influential psychologist of his time and was a supporter of Gauquelin's conclusions that planetary positions correlate with the personalities of eminent professionals. Professor Eysenck, along with another noted psychologist, Dr. David Nias,[8] wrote the following in 1982 about Gauquelin's work:

> *Because Gauquelin has, all along, published full details of his research in a series of documents, it is possible to evaluate independently the design and methods used in the research. This we have done, and we have been unable to find anything seriously wrong. On the contrary, we have been impressed by the meticulous care.*

Author and scholar John Anthony West, in his book *The Case for Astrology*, portrayed the Gauquelin findings as rock solid. He derided the stubborn scientists who refused to acknowledge them as being akin to the fabled cardinals who refused to peer down Galileo's telescope.

In 1987, eminent psychologist Suitbert Ertel, while visiting Gauquelin's "laboratory," happened to notice that as well as the published birth data of the 2888 eminent sportsmen, there were also 1503 unpublished, less eminent sportsmen. He was then startled to notice that in plotting the latter data in the normal way, by 36 sectors of Mars' diurnal circle, dips were obtained at the "key sectors," just where peaks occurred in the published data. Ertel published this finding[9] (Figure 3.2) in the *Journal of Scientific Exploration (JSE)*.

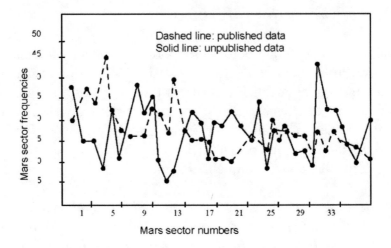

Figure 3.2: Ertel's plot of Gauquelin's published
and unpublished data

Ertel pooled together *all* of Gauquelin's eminent sportsmen data, both published and unpublished, obtaining a massive total of over four thousand, and plotted the percentages in Mars key sectors versus his arbitrary five "grades of eminence." The latter was the number of citations scored in five or six selected reference volumes (eminence rank 1—no score; rank 2—one score; rank 3—two scores, rank 4—three scores, rank 5—four or more scores). In statistical analysis, the smaller the size of the interval, the more accurate the analysis. As recalled from Table 3.1, interval size is the range of certain measurement values. The Gauquelins had simply divided the chart into 12 interval sizes (Figure 3.1), of which just two contained the predicted excess. Ertel divided the chart into 36 sectors. Using 36 sectors, there were 8 sectors with predicted excess and, therefore, a more precise analysis, giving a higher expected value. Ertel also used five grades of eminence—meaning the number of citations in five or six selected reference volumes (eminence rank 1 – no score, rank 2 – one score, rank 5 – four or more score). Figure 3.3 shows this for both the 12 and 36 key sectors with Mars' key sector percentages (kS%) versus the eminence. We can see from Figure 3.3 how Ertel's thirty-six sectors performed better than Gauquelin's twelve sectors[10].

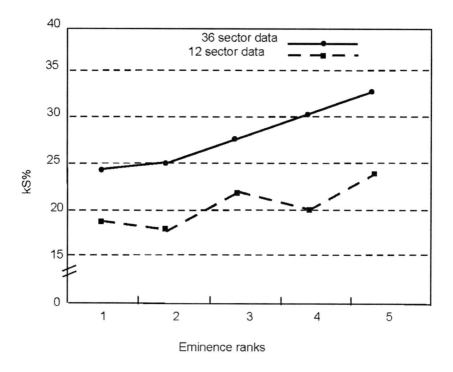

Figure 3.3: Mars key sector percentages

There have been three published replications by skeptical groups that wished to test Gauquelin's Mars effect with athletes: Belgian (1966), American (1980), and French (1996).[11] Each reported a negative result. Professor Ertel combined these three to get a total of 1668 sports champions of reliably known birth data, This total arises from adding the Belgian PARA Committee's 535 champions, the French CFEPP's (Comité Français pour l'Étude des Phénomènes Paranormaux) 1066 champions, and the U.S. skeptics' 408 champions (first two had considerable overlap).

He applied his eminence-grading protocol and thereby obtained a graph,[12] as shown in Figure 3.4, which indicates the Mars effect with prominent athletes. He included 1668 (= 512 + 509 + 260 + 172 + 102 + 113) sports champions of which 702 (= 208 + 208 + 111 + 75 + 46 + 54) had Mars in one of the four key sectors using a 36-sector division as indicated in Figure 3.4.

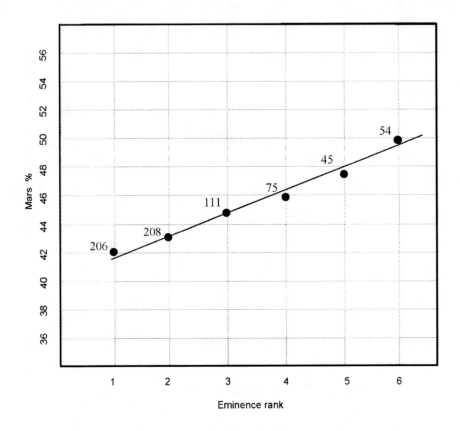

Figure 3.4: Ertel's graph with skeptics total of 1668

For physicians, Gauquelin used all members of the French Académie de Médecine (Academy of Medicine) of known birth data. Prof. Arno Muller discovered that a second edition of France's Academy of Medicine index was available, apparently unnoticed by Gauquelin. Muller and Ertel used it as a basis for rechecking the hypothesis. A collection of 1086 members of the Académie de Medicine of reliably known birth data was gathered, independent of the original Gauquelin collection, although overlapping with it.[13] It confirmed that the dominant effect was that of Saturn. The strong Mars presence also confirmed what Gauquelin had found in his first publication about the French physicians.

But the skeptics are still not satisfied. A good way to test this much-debated Mars effect, which is still going through anguished debate, would be to collect birth data of Olympic gold, silver, and bronze medalists every four years, collaborating with the skeptics in this endeavor. The criterion would be to ascertain that the champions did indeed have "the soul of hardened steel characteristic of the true sports champion," as Gauquelin put it,[14] wherein lies the Mars quality to be tested.

Other Works Based on Statistical Analysis

The association between the season of birth and a number of physical and psychological conditions has been firmly established. Research on schizophrenia and birth seasonality by E.F. Torrey, J. Rawlings Miller, and R. Yolken[15] has shown that individuals who later develop schizophrenia are more likely to have been born during January to April. Another study by Jayanti Chotai, Thomas Forgsen, Lars-Goran Nilsson, and Rolf Adolfsson[16] has shown that those born during February to April are more likely to have a novelty-seeking trait than those born during October to January.

The personality traits are not only likely to be influenced by genetic and environmental factors but also by astrological factors. Astrology relates a person's behavior and traits to the Sun sign, which corresponds to the person's month of birth. Pisces people (born between February 20 and March 20) have a martyr complex, alternating between optimism and pessimism; they are prone to depression. Aquarius people (born between January 21 and February 19) can be eccentric and dogmatic.

Kathy Yuan, Lu Zheng, and Qiaoqiao Zhu[17] of Michigan University investigated the relationship between lunar phases and stock market returns of forty-eight countries. Their findings indicate that the global stock returns are significantly lower during full Moon periods than new Moon periods. With all forty-eight countries included in the analysis, a statistically significant relationship is found between Moon phases and stock returns for both the fifteen-day and seven-day window specifications. Stock returns represent a combination of dividends and increases in the stock price, also known as capital gain. Yuan, Zheng, and Zhu found that the stock returns are, on average, 4 basis points (bps, equal to 1/100 of 1%) lower daily (about

5% annually) for the fifteen days around the full moon than for the fifteen days around the new Moon. Using a seven-day window, stock

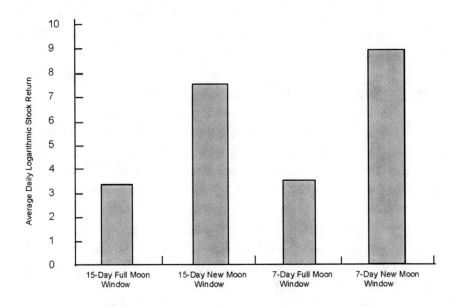

Figure 3.5: Average daily stock returns

returns are, on average, 6 bps lower daily (about 4%) on the full Moon days than on the new Moon days (Figure 3.5). Hence, the effect is stronger for the seven-day window specification than for the fifteen-day window specification. Another interesting observation is that the magnitude of this lunar effect is larger in the emerging market countries than in the developed countries.

They found that the lunar effect is stronger for stocks that are held mostly by individuals. This finding is consistent with the notion that lunar phases affect individual moods, which in turn affect investment behavior. They also found no evidence that the lunar effect observed in stock returns was associated with trading volumes or risk differentials during the full Moon and the new Moon periods. The lunar effect remained similar, after they controlled for other calendar-related anomalies, such as the January effect, the day-of-week effect, the calendar-month effect, and the holiday effect (including lunar holidays).

They also examined whether the lunar effect has any relation to stock capitalization. Large capitalization stocks have a higher percentage of institutional ownership than the small capitalization stocks. To assess the relation between lunar phases and stock capitalization, they formed ten stock portfolios based on market capitalization for stocks traded on the NYSE, AMEX, and NASDAQ. The estimated lunar effect was found stronger for NASDAQ stocks than for NYSE and AMEX stocks. Since investment decisions of individual investors are more likely to be affected by sentiments and mood than those of institutional investors, the lunar effect was found to be more pronounced in the pricing of small capitalization stocks. Overall, their study showed that stocks with more individual investor ownership displayed a stronger lunar effect, thus providing further evidence that mood or sentiment may affect asset prices. Their evidence indicated that the lunar effect cannot be explained away by macroeconomic announcements, common shocks in the stock markets, changes in short-term interest rates, day-of-the-week effect, or holiday effect.

In a statistical analysis of hundred of earthquakes, Brian T. Johnston[18] reported that earthquakes appear more likely to occur as planets approach major aspects to each other. Johnston used precise data from the U.S. Geological Survey, mainly between the years 1996 and 2000. An aspect in astrology is the relationship between two planets, expressed in degrees and minutes at the birth moment. This relationship can be benefic or malefic and is very important for astrology analysis. Johnston found that seismic activity is significantly associated with major aspects, and it appears to support the traditional astrological association between applying aspects and the timing of critical events.

Noted astrologer Judith Hill and Jacalyn Thompson studied the link between naturally red-haired subjects and Mars.[19] Their statistical analysis found that naturally red-haired people were more likely to be born with Mars within 30 degrees of the ascendant and not within 30 degrees of the descendant. Their findings have been replicated using hundreds of accurate time-of-birth data from different countries. This evidence supports the traditional associations of Mars with red hair and the ascendant with physical appearance.

Sara Ridgley[20] found from statistical analysis that workplace accidents were significantly more frequent around days when the Sun is in conjunct (0 degrees), opposite (180 degrees), or square (90 degrees) to the Sun's exact position in the birth charts of the injured workers. Ridgley conducted a study of over a thousand people living in California who filed workers compensation claims and were disabled for at least three months. A follow-up study, however, of a similar database of work-related injuries in Sweden failed to replicate the results of the California study, with the least of the accidents around the birthday (conjunction), due to the fact that Swedish workers get their birthdays off work. Ridgely suspects that the differences in results might stem from "very different cultural values and psychological attitudes toward work, people in authority, and the individual's self-worth."[21]

Concluding Remarks

Starting with Michel Gauquelin, many leading researchers in the scientific field have used statistical analysis for astrology research. They have understood the statistical potential of astrology and have published evidence of correlations between astrological patterns and earthly events, behavior, and character. But there needs to be much more work in this area to establish astrology on a firm scientific footing and convince the skeptics of its place as a science. The first thing needed is a birth chart based on accurate birth time. Secondly, there should be a minimum of interpretation errors in the birth chart. Different astrologers have different interpretations of the same birth chart. Currently, astrologers do not generally share their knowledge—this is where the astrology societies have a large part to play. A common benchmark for interpretation of birth charts should be worked out by the expert astrologers. Astrologers typically do not get any feedback from their clients; thus, they do not have any method of modifying or improving their knowledge and technique.

Collection of data and statistical analysis of collected data are essential in this respect. There should be a central databank where all practicing astrologers and consultants should enter the information of their clients. The information should include (a) the Sun sign versus the character and feature of the client, (b) planet positions versus the character and feature of the client, (c) planet aspects versus the character and feature of the client, (d) methods of astrology prediction, and (e) astrology predictions for the client and the results after follow-up with the client. A panel of experts assigned by the astrological community should interpret the data and modify the benchmark accordingly.

Finally, although scientific proofs and analyses are required to establish astrology on a firmer scientific basis, it is the experience of human life with celestial bodies that will bring astrology closer to truth.

> *The skeptic will say, "It may well be true that this system of equations is reasonable from a logical standpoint. But this does not prove that it corresponds to nature." You are right, dear skeptic. Experience alone can decide on truth. ... Pure logical thinking cannot yield us any knowledge of the empirical world: all knowledge of reality starts from experience and ends in it.*

—Albert Einstein (1954)

Chapter 4
Astrology is Social Science

Astrology represents a summation of all psychological knowledge of antiquity. And astrology is, if well used, a splendid method that can lead to deeper self knowledge and personal growth.

—Carl Jung

In this chapter, we will discuss the second good reason why astrology is science: astrology is social science. Social science comprises academic disciplines concerned with the study of the social life of human groups and individuals, including anthropology, economics, education, human geography, political science, psychology, and social study. Anthropology deals with the aspects of the humanities and human biology. Economics is a social science that seeks to analyze and describe the production, distribution, and consumption of wealth. Education encompasses teaching and learning of specific skills and imparting of knowledge and wisdom. Human geography focuses on how humans influence the environment they occupy. Political science is a discipline that deals with the theory and practice of politics. Psychology is a field involving the study of behavior and mental processes. Social study is concerned with social problems, their causes, their solutions, and their human aspects.

Social sciences are largely observational, in that the explanations for cause/effect relationships are largely subjective. Similarly, astrology is also observational—the motion and position of the celestial objects in the sky are related to the character and situation of a person. Astrology provides insight into a person's character, traits, and personal strengths and weaknesses, based on the person's birth chart. The astrologer obtains the data by analyzing the Sun sign, planet positions in the houses and Zodiacs, and planet aspects in the person's birth chart. Psychologists gather insight into the character of the client by having prolonged discussions with the client, with probing questions and answers. From the data derived from the session, the psychologist can determine the strengths and weaknesses of the client and prescribe suitable treatment. In this chapter, insight is given into how astrology, psychology, and social science can study and analyze a person's character and behavior, and how these areas of science can support each other. Astrology extends the span of social science to celestial objects, relating to human behavior and action. Social science comprises academic disciplines concerned with the study of the social life of human groups and individuals, including anthropology, economics, geography, history, political science, psychology, and social studies.

Statistical Analysis of Social Science

Statistics and statistical analyses have become a key feature of contemporary social science. Statistics have been, perhaps, most important in economics and psychology, which have incorporated and relied primarily on statistical analyses as a method of argument for decades. Let us consider a simple example to see how statistical analysis can be used for the following topic: the influence of participation in athletics on the moral character of children.

For the exercise, we question one hundred parents, and their responses are given in Table 4.1.

Table 4.1: Responses of 100 parents

Response	Frequency of response
Strong positive influence	35
Some positive influence	40
No influence	15
Slight negative influence	8
Strong negative influence	2

With the data so organized, we can make a descriptive statement as follows: 75 of 100 parents (or 75%) viewed participation in athletics as having a positive influence on the moral character of children. Because astrology is also based on statistical analysis, the technique used in social science and astrology is similar.

Astrology and Psychology

Psychology is concerned with the mental processes and behavior of a person. Psychologists study such phenomena as perception, cognition, emotion, personality, behavior, and interpersonal relationships. Psychology also refers to the application of such knowledge to various spheres of human activity, including issues related to daily life (e.g., family, education, and work) and the treatment of mental health problems. Psychologists attempt to understand the role of these functions in individual and social behavior, while also exploring the underlying physiological and neurological processes.

Astrology can be better understood if it can be compared with the theories of personality and behavior from psychology and social sciences. These theories can be described in terms of values, skills, beliefs, love, urges, and development.[22] Astrology can relate to these terms with the environment of signs, planets, and aspects.

Values could be (a) me-directed, putting personal ambition, feelings, and needs above every thing else, (b) us-directed, sharing with family or community above all, (c) you-directed, closely associating with partner or friend above all, and (d) them-directed, putting public organization above all. According to astrology, people with the Sun signs Capricorn, Aquarius, and Pisces tend to show values between me-directed and them-directed; Aries, Taurus, and Gemini people tend to show values between me-directed and us-directed; Cancer, Leo, and Virgo people tend to show values between us-directed and you-directed; Libra, Scorpio, and Sagittarius people tend to show values between you-directed and them-directed.

Skills could be classified into the following: lead, compete, cooperate, and follow. One can either lead or follow, compete or cooperate. According to astrology, the tenth, eleventh, and twelfth houses indicate skills with a mixture of lead and compete. The seventh, eighth, and ninth houses indicate skills with a mixture of lead and cooperate. The fourth, fifth, and sixth houses indicate skills with a mixture of cooperate and follow. The first, second, and third houses indicate a mixture of compete and follow.

In psychology and social sciences, beliefs are associated with emotional intelligence, which consists of self-confidence, self-reliance, self-restraint, and self-discipline. In astrology, the aspects of the planets show the degree of alignment the planets make with each other. The simplified versions of the aspects are the conjunction, waxing square, opposition, and waning square. A square aspect is waxing if it occurs before the opposition point (180 degrees), and it is waning if it takes place after the opposition. In the more familiar terms of the Sun and Moon phases, these four aspects are represented by the new, first quarter, full, and last quarter phases, respectively. According to astrology, a waning square after conjunction indicates self-discipline; a waxing square before conjunction indicates self-confidence; a waning square after opposition indicates self-restraint; a waxing square before opposition indicates self-reliance.

In psychology or social sciences, love is classified as physical, possessive, flirtatious, practical, affectionate, or unselfish. In astrology, the horizon axis (the line connecting the ascendant and descendant) represents the relationship of equality, because the horizon is where all things are on the same physical level. The horizon axis intercepts two Zodiacal signs, one in the east and one in the west. This means that there are six pairs of opposing horizon signs. Although the signs in these pairs oppose each other, each pair has common attributes that balance its opposition to express a love relationship. According to astrology, an Aries/Libra pair represents physical love; a Taurus/Scorpio pair represents possessive love; a Gemini/Sagittarius pair represents flirtatious love; a Cancer/Capricorn pair represents practical love; a Leo/Aquarius pair represents affectionate love; a Virgo/Pisces pair represents unselfish love.

In psychology, urges are classified as showing, consuming, moving, bonding, speeding, gaining, reducing, testing, hiding, and extracting. Astrology suggests that the planets represent inner urges. Hence, according to astrology, the Sun represents showing, the Moon represents consuming, Mercury represents moving, Venus represents bonding, Mars represents speeding, Jupiter represents gaining, Saturn represents reducing, Uranus represents testing, Neptune represents hiding, and Pluto represents extracting.

In astrology, developmental patterns are mostly made by the slower-moving planets—Jupiter, Saturn, Uranus, and Neptune—as they transit the four major aspects to their original positions at the time of birth. Thus, these transiting planets can conjoin, wax a square, oppose, or wane a square to its natal position. Because the planetary speed is the same, they occur at approximately the same ages for every person. The exception is Pluto, whose orbit is so elongated that aspects to its natal position can occur at noticeably at different ages for different persons. If the planets represent urges and have a dependency on their natal configurations, then each of these aspects should result in self-conflicting beliefs in identity. According to astrology, the time periods that are considered to be problematic tend to be when people are at ages fourteen, twenty-tone, twenty-nine, forty-two, fifty-nine, sixty-five, eighty-three, and eighty-eight. Coming-of-age transitions in developmental psychology appear to compare favorably with the astrological developmental patterns.

Psychological Astrology

A renewed interest in astrology developed in the twentieth century with the involvement of certain important figures; Swiss psychologist Carl Jung (1875–1961) stands out among them. Jung developed his distinctive approach to the study of human mind, called Jungian psychology. The human mind has both conscious and unconscious parts. Reliable communication between the conscious and unconscious parts is necessary for the wholeness of a person. Encounter with the unconscious is done through mystical symbols, called archetypes, according to Jung. Essential to the encounter with the unconscious and the reconciliation of the individual's consciousness with the broader world is learning these archetypes.

Jungian psychology distinguishes between personal and collective unconscious. The collective unconscious contains archetypes common to all human beings. Just as all humans have a common physical heritage (like having a heart, a stomach, two hands, etc.), so do all humans have innate psychological archetypes, which compose the collective unconscious.

Jung believed that a lot can be learned about the human psyche through astrology, not only because the stars and planets are an external reflection of our inner selves but also because the inherently symbolic nature of astrology allows us to consciously correlate symbols with the unconscious knowledge. Astrology is a language of symbols that mediates between the conscious and unconscious. Jung believed that the connection between the celestial bodies and the individual is acausal and synchronistic.[23]

Jung associated different archetypes with specific planets and strongly believed that the birth chart of a person would tell the psyche of the person by generating archetypal images. He frequently looked at the birth charts of his patients and believed that the symbols in the chart made useful suggestions about that patient's psyche from the collective unconscious.

Psychological astrology or astropsychology is a reformulation of contemporary astrology within terms of psychological concepts and practices. The core feature of psychological astrology is its application to growth, development, and actualization of human potential[24]. Contemporary astrology was limited to trait descriptions, fate, and predictions of good and bad times. Psychological astrology deals with the inner awareness of a person leading to psychological development. Human consciousness is progressively evolving from lower to higher states. Psychological astrology empowers humans to actualize latent potentials rather than predicting what is going to happen, or whether one can expect good or bad life. Hence, the primary directive for psychological astrology is supporting individual's growth and development.

Psychological astrology deals with the relation between subjective and objective reality, which Jung called "synchronicity," the confluence of inner and outer events. This relationship between inner and outer, subjective and objective, and the process of feedback activates higher level of psyche over time.

Psychological astrology transforms psychology to a more spiritualized model that links psyche to cosmos and reconnects humanity to divine heritage. In so doing, it challenges the presumption of psychology that consciousness is the phenomenon of biological and social determinisms.

One notable quote of Carl Jung on astrology is given below:

> *Since you want to know my opinion about astrology, I can*
> *tell you that I've been interested in this particular activity*
> *of the human mind for more than thirty years. As I am*
> *a psychologist, I am chiefly interested in the particular*
> *light the horoscope sheds on certain complications in the*
> *character. In cases of difficult psychological diagnosis I*
> *usually get a horoscope in order to have a further point*
> *of view from an entirely different angle. I must say that*
> *I very often found that the astrological data elucidated*
> *certain points, which I otherwise would have been unable*
> *to understand. From such experiences I formed the opinion*
> *that astrology is of particular interest to the psychologist,*
> *since it contains a sort of psychological experience*
> *which we call "projected"—this means that we find the*
> *psychological facts as it were in the constellations.*

—letter to astrologer B.V. Raman, September 6, 1947

Professor Hans Jungen Eysenck became interested in astrology after the findings of Michel Gauquelin. He believed that there are links between planetary positions and personalities. Encouraged by the interest of Eysenck in astrology, astro-sympathizers organized three research seminars at Long Beach in California, Freiburg in Germany, and Naples in Italy in 1986, 1987, and 1988, respectively. The first seminar resulted in the formation of the Committee for Objective Research in Astrology (CORA) with Eysenck as the chairman and twelve others (academics and astrologers) who had particular expertise. CORA was set up to counter the generally poor quality of astrological research by providing free advice and guidance.

In the late 1970s, Eysenck and David Nias started research in the area of scientific evidence for astrology, aimed more at the general public. This resulted in their writing the book *Astrology: Science or Superstition?* (1982), which covered astrological principles, Sun signs, marriage, illness, suicide, appearance, time twins, season of birth, terrestrial and solar cycles, radio propagation, earthquakes, lunar effects, and the work of Gauquelin.[25]

Psychological Effect of the Moon

Lunar phases affect mood and behavior. The Moon has been associated with mental disorder since ancient times, which is reflected by the word "lunacy," derived from Luna, the Roman goddess of the Moon. Popular belief links the full Moon to higher incidence of epilepsy, crime, suicide, mental illness, disaster, accidents, births, and fertility.

Biological evidence suggests that lunar phases have an impact on the human body and behavior. A woman's menstrual cycle follows a similar pattern to a lunar cycle, which suggests the influence of the Moon. Studies by S.P. Law[26] found a synchronous relationship between the menstrual cycle and the lunar phases. Studies also find a lunar effect on fertility; Criss and Marcum[27] reported that births vary systematically over lunar cycles, with peak fertility during the third lunar quarter. Lunar phases also affect human nutrient intake. De Castro and Pearcey[28] documented an 8% increase in meal size and a 26% decrease in alcohol intake at the time of a full Moon.

Much attention has been paid to the lunar effect on human

mood and behavior in psychology literature. Neal and Colledge[29] documented an increase in general-practice consultations during the full Moon phase. Lieber[30] reported that a disproportionately higher number of criminal offenses occur during the full Moon phase; Tasso and Miller[31] reported similar results. Weiskott[32] reported evidence that the number of crisis calls is higher during full Moon and waning phases. Hicks-Caskey and Potter[33] suggested an effect of the day of a full Moon on the acting-out behavior of developmentally delayed, institutionalized women.

Overall, the effect of the Moon has been studied informally and formally for years. However, despite the attention this effect has received, psychological evidence for the lunar hypothesis, in general, is not conclusive, even though biological evidence is strong. Campbell and Beets[34] concluded from their empirical studies that lunar phases have little effect on psychiatric hospital admissions, suicides, or homicides. But, some researchers argue that this lack of relationship does not preclude a lunar effect.[35] It may simply mean that the effect has not been adequately tested due to small sample sizes and short sample time periods. Moreover, the psychology literature has mainly focused on trying to link the Moon's phases to extreme behavioral problems in a few disturbed people, rather than a less drastic effect on human beings in general.

In addition, survey evidence suggests a wide belief in the lunar effect. Rotton and Kelly[36] found that 49.4% of the respondents to their survey believe in lunar phenomena. Among psychiatric nurses, this percentage rises to 74%[37]. Danzl[38] found survey evidence that suggests that 80% of the nurses and 64% of the physicians in the emergency department believe that Moon cycles affect patients. Scientific explanations have been proposed to account for the Moon's effect on the brain: sleep deprivation, heavy nocturnal dew, tidal effect, weather patterns, magnetism and polarization of the Moon's light.[39,40,41,42]

Given the extensive documentation of the correlation between lunar phases and human feelings, thoughts, and behaviors—more specifically, the correlation between the full Moon periods and sleep deprivation, depressed mood, and suicidal events—the hypothesis in this study is that investors may value financial assets less during full

Moon periods than during new Moon periods, due to the changes in mood associated with lunar phases.

Astrology and Twins

Often, we hear that if astrology really works, then why don't twins, who are born at the same time, have the same life, characteristics, and traits? There are two types of twins: birth twins and time twins. Birth twins have the same parents, and time twins are born at the same time but have different parents. There are two types of birth twins: fraternal, or dizygotic, and identical, or monozygotic. Fraternal twins result from two separate fertilized ova. Identical twins result from one fertilized ovum that splits into two. Fraternal twins share only 50% of their genes. Hence, the two individuals are no more alike than any two brothers or sisters. Identical twins have identical gene material, or DNA. The makeup of DNA is called genotype; human characteristics are determined by phenotype, based on the expression of DNA. It is usually based on a complex interaction of several genes. Identical twins do not have identical fingerprints.

Traits determined by phenotype, such as fingerprints, physical appearances, and others are the interaction of the individual's genes and the development environment in the uterus. Thus, a DNA test cannot determine the difference between identical twins, while a simple fingerprint can. Some identical twins in the womb share a placenta. One twin may have a more advantageous connection to the placenta, receiving the first run of the nutrients. Also, twin-to-twin transfusion syndrome (TTTS) is another condition that affects twins in the womb and impacts their development. TTTS is a condition in pregnancy where blood passes disproportionately between twins in a shared placenta.

Characters or traits of a child are caused by three factors:[43]

1. Time of birth: accurate birth chart by astrology provides the data

2. Environment: family and society

3. Genes: provided by the parents

To what extent each of the above three factors contributes to make up the total traits or characteristics of a child is not known. But the astrological birth chart is certainly a contributing factor, as used by astrologers, psychologists, and alternative medicine practitioners.

Concluding Remarks

A special genre of testing the validity of astrology has been developed, mainly by astrology skeptics. These tests are based on one-to-one matching, which means that a specific question must have a specific answer. Hence, the results of these tests are not encouraging and cause disbelief in astrology. A word of caution is warranted here. A one-to-one matching test requires a one-to-one relationship that assumes a high or even complete level of determinism. But astrological tests need to be statistically based, where a large number of samples should be evaluated to find a correlation for a certain feature, instead of a one-to-one match. Secondly, astrologers should follow benchmarks to interpret results of their analyses to avoid interpretative errors. Astrology is a branch of social science and should be practiced in a way similar to psychology and other branches of social science, based on statistical evaluation and benchmarks.

Social sciences like astrology are sometimes criticized as being less scientific than the natural sciences, in that they are seen as less rigorous or empirical in their methods. This claim is commonly made when comparing social sciences to fields such as physics, chemistry, or biology, in which corroboration of data is far more incisive with regard to data obtained from specifically designed experiments. Social sciences and astrology are observational, in that the explanations for a cause-and-effect relationship is subjective. Social science and astrology are best practiced as phronesis, which focuses on four value questions: (1) Where are we going? (2) Who gains and who loses? (3) Is this development desirable? (4) What should we do about it? Natural science is best practiced as episteme, which is the "apparatus" to establish a scientific theory. Both have important but different roles to play in the society.

The social world and astrological world are much too complex to be studied as one would study molecules and cells. The actions of molecules or chemical substances are always the same when placed in certain situations. Humans and society, on the other hand, do not have certain rules that always have the same outcome, and they cannot guarantee to react the same way to certain situations.

Astrology is another branch of social science with similar analysis techniques as are used in other branches of social science, but it studies the subjective relationship between humans and celestial bodies. Astrology cannot be studied with the methodologies of natural science, thus astrology is viewed as a pseudoscience because of the failure of pursuing such methodologies. Astrology should be treated as another branch of social science.

The only function of economic forecasting is to make astrology look respectable.

—John Galbraith

Chapter 5
Astrology is Linked with Alternative Medicine

He who does not understand astrology is not a doctor but a fool.

—Hippocrates

In this chapter, I will discuss the third good reason why astrology is a science: astrology is linked with alternative medicine. I will describe how the various branches of alternative medicine relate to astrology and complement each other.

Alternative medicine has been defined as preventive or therapeutic health-care practices, such as ayurveda, homeopathy, traditional Chinese medicine, acupuncture, yoga, tai chi, reiki, chiropractic, etc. Alternative medicine is different from mainstream conventional Western medical methods, which are predominantly used in all countries. However, the use of alternative medicine is increasing. A recent survey by the National Center for Complementary and Alternative Medicine (NCCAM) in the U.S. in 2002 showed that 50% of adults aged 18 years and older in the U.S. used some form of alternative medicine. Other studies indicate that many people use alternative medicine in conjunction with conventional medicine.

In ancient times, people theorized that illness was the result of imbalances of vital energy in the body. In different cultures, this vital energy was interpreted as prana, chi, ki, etc., as described earlier. In India, sages tapped into ayurveda 10,000 years ago; it was put into writing in the Vedas around 5000 years ago. Ancient qigong masters in China developed tai chi and traditional Chinese medicine 3000 years ago. In the fifth century BCE, the Greek physician Hippocrates developed the concept of black bile, yellow bile, blood, and phlegm as the four humors. Ancient people considered body, mind, and spirit as part of the whole human being. The aim was to keep these forces in balance. Medical practice was based on diet, exercise, herbs, and massage.

Development of Western Medicine

In the West, the medical treatment remained unchanged for 2000 years after the death of Hippocrates. The development of conventional medical science started after the Industrial Revolution in the West. With the development of technology, scientists learned more about individual body parts and systems. Body was separated from mind and spirit. Many doctors concentrated on specific body parts and systems. Medicinal practice became more specialized.

Conventional or Western medicine got a real boost from the work of three eighteenth-century scientists: Louis Pasteur, Joseph Lister, and Robert Koch. These three scientists discovered that microorganisms, such as bacteria, cause all infections and some diseases. The French scientist Louis Pasteur developed the "germ theory" of disease. He also developed pasteurization and a method of vaccination against rabies. English surgeon Joseph Lister introduced carbolic acid (phenol) to sterilize surgical instruments and to clean wounds. German physician Robert Koch isolated tubercle bacillus (tuberculosis) and vibrio cholerae (cholera).

The twentieth century was a golden century for Western medicine. Antibiotics were discovered in 1930s, providing real cures for fatal diseases such as tuberculosis and pneumonia. More vaccines were developed for polio and smallpox. New surgical techniques were developed, such as heart bypass surgery and organ transplants. New medical techniques, like MRI, allowed physician to see the inside of the body.

Western conventional medicine is excellent for acute illnesses and wounds but is less effective for treating chronic and degenerative diseases. When someone has a serious accident, conventional medical practice can immediately treat them with surgery and medicine. Acute illnesses have a rapid onset and a short, serious course. Examples are heart attack, malaria, cholera, and appendicitis. Conventional medicine can treat them well, but chronic diseases, although not immediately life-threatening, last for a long time and recur repeatedly and frequently. Examples are arthritis, asthma, migraine, and back pain. Degenerative diseases cause gradual deterioration of organs and tissues, leading ultimately to fatality. Examples are heart disease, cancer, respiratory disease, kidney disease, etc. Alternative medicine is proving very beneficial in treating chronic and degenerative diseases.

Conventional medical treatment often does not go to the root causes of the diseases; it mainly suppresses the symptoms with drugs. Patients suffering from blood pressure are prescribed beta blockers to keep their blood pressure in check. But this does not address the root cause of the problem. Doctors who practice conventional medicine often focus only on a certain organ or area of the body without considering the whole body and health of the patient. Alternative medicine always addresses the root cause of the disease; hence, it is slow but sure. Alternative medicine does not focus only on a single organ or area of the body; it considers that the function of an organ is dependent on the function of the whole body. When a water pipe in a house bursts in cold weather, merely changing the pipe may temporarily solve the problem, but it is going to burst again. Only by insulating the house properly can the problem be permanently solved. This is the approach of alternative medicine.

Another common complaint against conventional medicine is the relationship between the doctors and patients. Too many conventional medical doctors treat the patients like machines, rather than human beings with feelings. They simply do not spend time listening to the patients but depend totally on the test results of diagnostic tools and machines. This makes diagnosis inadequate because of the limitation of these test tools. Second—and more important—a lot can be learned about the symptoms and causes of the disease from discussions with the patients. After all, faith on the doctor can only improve the result of treatment. Alternative medicine makes the patients active partners in the treatment by encouraging placebo effect, whereby the patients' conditions improve simply because they believe that they are being helped.

Conventional medical treatment and drugs are becoming very expensive. Many people who do not have medical insurance or sufficient money are finding it very difficult to undergo treatment. The main complaint is against the drug companies, who many people believe are making money unjustifiably. Alternative medicine is not expensive and rarely has any side effect.

Merits of Alternative Medicine

Although alternative medicine started to fall out of favor in late 1880s due to the successful progress made by conventional Western medicine, today it is enjoying a comeback. Although the traditional medical community may complain that alternative medicine is not scientifically tested and proven, 50% of all adults in the U.S. use alternative medicine. Many people turn to alternative medicine after conventional medical treatments have failed to help them. Many people use mainstream medicine for diagnosis and basic information and then turn to alternative medicine for what they believe to be health-enhancing measures. A growing number of medical colleges offer courses in alternative medicine. For example, the University of Arizona College of Medicine offers a program in integrative medicine, which trains physicians in various branches of alternative medicine. Alternative medicine is being categorized together with complementary medicine, using the umbrella term complementary and alternative medicine, or CAM.

Ayurveda and Astrology

Ayurveda, the oldest known alternative medicine, originated in India. Ayurveda is derived from the Sanskrit word *ayus* (life) and *veda* (science or knowledge). Ayurveda recognizes a life force called prana, which flows in the body through subtle channels, called *nadis*. There are more than 72,000 *nadis* in the human body. According to ayurveda, all of the nature is made up of five elements: space, earth, air, fire, and water. When these elements are charged with prana, they combine to form the three doshas, Dosha is the ayurvedic mind and body type. Space and air combine to form the Vata dosha; fire and water together form the Pitta dosha; water and earth combine to form the Kapha dosha.

The balance and unbalance among the three doshas[44] determine the state of our health. When the doshas are perfectly balanced, we are in perfect health and mind. When any of the doshas is unbalanced, our system goes erratic and sick. Each of the doshas controls different aspects of our being and is located in particular areas of the body.

The Vata dosha controls the circulation of breath and blood, menstruation, and the entire nervous system. Vata resides primarily in the colon. It is considered the important dosha, and its imbalance can lead to greatest number of diseases. Vata people are lean, quite short or very tall, and underweight. They have dry skin, lips, and tongues, and split ends in their hair, and nails that break easily. They are sensitive to cold and wind and like a warmer climate. They have poor digestion and a tendency to have gas. They do not cope well with intense physical challenge and stress. They have intense interest in initiating sex, but are quickly sated. Balanced Vata persons are very imaginative, creative, and visionary. They have the ability to learn and grasp things easily. They love to travel, making it difficult for them to maintain any kind of stability. But unbalanced Vata persons are hyperactive with unclear minds and erratic memories. Typical Vata ailments include constipation, gas, arthritis, sore throats, and headaches.

Pitta controls the metabolism, hormones, and the digestive system. Pitta powers the intellect, thoughts, ideas, and emotions. It is located in the stomach and small intestine. Pitta persons are of medium body size and generally slim. They have oily and freckled skin and are prone to acne and rashes. They have a strong appetite with good digestion. They have a hot body temperature and dislikes heat. They have abundant energy, with a sharp memory and logical minds. They are hardworking and generally successful. Unbalanced Pitta people can be impatient, irritable, angry, stubborn, and opinionated. At their worst, they can be a control freak and fanatical. Typical problems with aggravated Pittas are ulcers, heartburn, acidity, and insomnia.

Kapha is responsible for the creation and strength of all body structures, including bones, muscles, tissues, and fats. Kapha resides in the stomach, chest, throat, head, and lymph nodes. It is considered the most stable of the doshas. Kapha people have large, strong, and well-developed bodies. They are sensitive to cold and damp and like warm and sunny places. They have great deal of capacity for intense physical activities. They are loving, affectionate, kind, gentle, and highly tolerant people. They are slow and steady in most activities. They are slow learners but retain information once it is learned. When in balance, they have strong immunity. Unbalanced Kapha people can become greedy, possessive, and depressed. Physical problems that arise with aggravated Kaphas include asthma, hay fever, flu, sinus headaches, and allergies. Extreme conditions of Kapha may lead to diabetes and heart attack.

Prana is derived from the combination of two Sanskrit words, *pra*, or first unit, and *na*, or energy. Prana is the life energy. Pranayama is another Sanskrit word, which means *ayama*, or the expansion or manifestation of prana. Pranayama is practiced by the control of breath. Prana is in all things, whether animate or inanimate. It is the energy essence of the air we breathe. In human life, the energy of prana includes both physical and mental energies that sustain both body and mind. Prana is the force that holds together the elements of the body and assists in the cohesion of the atomic particles of the body. Prana is the cause of all functions of the body and mind. If Prana recedes from any part of the body, that part loses its function.

A chakra in Indian culture is a center of activity that receives, assimilates, and expresses life-force energy. The word chakra literally translates as wheel or disk. Chakras are energy centers in the body, located at major branchings of the human nervous system, beginning at the base of the spinal column and moving upward to the top of the skull. Chakras are considered to be a point, or nexus, of metaphysical and/or biophysical energy of the human body. Six of these wheels are stacked in a column of energy that spans from the base of the spine to the middle of the forehead; a seventh is beyond the physical region. It is the six major chakras that correlate with basic states of consciousness.

According to ayurveda, doshas become unbalanced due to improper diet, negative emotions and stress, and unhealthful lifestyles. Hence, the doshas can be balanced by proper food, regular exercise, and a positive lifestyle with a healthy body, mind, and spirit. Unbalanced doshas create *amas* (toxins) in the body. When the *amas* become excessive, they clog the *nadis* of the body, blocking the flow of prana in the body and resulting in disease.

Ayurveda is taught in a number of reputable schools and universities in India. Ayurveda is not recognized as a legitimate system of medicine in the West. In the United States, Bastyr University is offering doctoral program in Ayurveda.

The Sanskrit term for Indian or Vedic astrology is *jyotish*. The derivation of the word Jyotish from its syllables is the following: *Jaya* (birth, *O* (and), *Ta* (Earth or stars), and *Ish* (knowledgable).The word jyotish means knowledge of birth in relation to the stars and Earth.

Ayurvedic treatises—the Sushrita Samhita and Chakra Samhita—were written five thousand years ago. They contained a wealth of information with regard to cause of disease, noting the vitiation of the natural elements that surround the human body. While ayurveda looks at the natural elements as the root of the human disease, astrology scours the celestial bodies. According to astrology, the movements of the planets and stars have an effect on the body. The planets could be malefic or benefic. Hence, if the malefic planets are present in the wrong houses or Zodiacs, they can cause disease in the human body.

Ayurveda deals with earthly elements, and astrology deals with celestial bodies. Both of these, if vitiated, can have a negative effect on the human body. This is the scope under which both ayurveda and astrology perform. Ayurveda provides treatment to remedy the diseases, and astrology provides suggestions to correct the effect of the harmful positions of planets. In certain cases, astrologists would prescribe some ayurvedic preparation in order to reduce or totally eliminate the malefic effect of the planets. Similarly, ayurvedic *vaidyas* (doctors) would make a detailed study of the horoscope of the patient before deciding on a treatment. In this way, ayurveda and astrology complement each other. They are branches of the same overall kind of treatment in the ancient Indian tradition.

Whether the diseases are simple—coughs, cold, fever, constipation—or very complicated type—diabetes, hypertension, cardiovascular diseases, mental problems—they can be treated over time with an effective balance of astrology and ayurveda. Astrology will ascertain which planets have malefic impact, and ayurveda will prescribe an herb to remove the malefic impact of the planets, as well as correct the vitiation of the doshas.

In Indian astrology, there are nine planets, called *navagrahas*, derived from the combination of the words *nava* (nine) and *graha* (planet). Similar to Western astrology, the Sun and Moon are considered as planets, but the distant planets Uranus, Neptune, and Pluto are not included. Instead, the Indian astrology includes the north lunar node, called Rahu, and the south lunar node, called Ketu. These are portrayed as the head and tail, respectively, of a banished demon in the space. Indian mythology describes Rahu and Ketu as a snake demon who went to drink the nectar of immortality, which only divine beings were allowed to consume. The Sun and the Moon witnessed this and announced it to God Vishnu, who then cut the demon in half. Because the demon had already drunk some nectar, however, it was transformed to an immortal being. As a concession to the demon, a place with the planets in the heavenly function was granted, provoking the solar and lunar eclipses. The function of the two parts of demon is to make every being face his shadows and unresolved past karmas. The navagrahas are the Sun, the Moon, Mars, Mercury, Jupiter, Venus, Saturn, Rahu, and Ketu. The Indian horoscope chart is called kundali. The grahas (planets) are very influential in a person's kundali. These navagrahas determine various aspects of a person's body. Indian astrology has studied the correlation of the navagrahas with different spiritual and physical aspects of a person. The effect of the nine planets on a person, according to Indian astrology, is given in Table 5.1.

Table 5.1: Effect of the Navagrahas

Planets (grahas)	Western name	Parts represented
Surya	Sun	Soul
Chandra	Moon	Mind
Mangala	Mars	Vitality
Budha	Mercury	Nerves
Brihaspati	Jupiter	Heart
Shukra	Venus	Sex organs
Shani	Saturn	Feet, muscles
Rahu	North Lunar Node	Bones
Ketu	South Lunar Node	Secret parts

Diseases attributed to the navagrahas are as follows:

1. The Sun represents the human soul. Hence, the Sun is the master of the human body. If the position of the Sun is strong in the person's kundali, then the person's body composition would be strong.

2. The Moon represents a person's mind. Hence, if the position of the Moon is strong in a person's kundali, then the person would have a balanced mind, without mental problems. If the Moon is weak, then the person will suffer from mental disorders.

3. Mars is a hot planet. If the position of Mars in a kundali is weak, then the person will be prone to catching viruses that cause various diseases.

4. A weak Mercury in kundali causes nervous problems.

5. A weak Jupiter in kundali causes heart problem. A strong Jupiter is an essential element in a person's well-being.

6. A strong Venus in kundali causes a good love life and sex life.

7. Saturn is the biggest cause of diseases in the human body. Most human diseases are caused by the prevalence of Saturn in the kundali.

8. Rahu can cause a sudden, unexpected setback in a person's life. It is generally malefic.

9. Ketu is called a hidden planet and also can cause an unexpected setback in a person's life.

Ayurveda without astrology—and astrology without ayurveda—is incomplete. In order to make full use of these two areas, there needs to be more research to obtain the full benefit of treatment for the human body and mind. Hippocrates, the father of modern medicine said:

> *A physician without the knowledge of astrology has no right to call himself a physician.*

This kind of belief was reiterated by Dr. Kallman of the Psychiatric Institute at New York, who said:

> *Every being has a clock set at the moment of his/her birth, which predetermines illnesses and accidents.*

Yoga and Astrology

Yoga, which in Sanskrit means "union," is a group of ancient spiritual practices originating in India around 3000 BCE. It focuses on altering the state of a person's mind to generate healing within the body. Hindu scriptures that discuss different aspects of yoga include the Upanishads, the Bhagavad-Gita, the Yoga Sutras of Patanjali, the Hatha Yoga Pradipika, the Shiva Samhita, and many others. Major branches of yoga include: Hatha yoga, Karma yoga, Jnana yoga, Bhakti yoga, and Raja yoga.

Traditional Hatha yoga is a holistic yogic path that includes moral disciplines, asanas (postures), pranayama (breath control), and meditation. The Hatha yoga predominantly practiced in the West consists mostly of asanas and exercise. The other branch of yoga that focuses on the physical culture is the Raja yoga. Both of these are commonly referred to as Ashtanga yoga—yoga of eight parts (*ashta*, meaning eight, and *anga*, meaning limbs). The eight limbs are yama and niyama, which are ethical obligations; asana and pranayama, which are breath control; pratyahara, which is sense withdrawal; dharana, which is concentration; dhyana, which is meditation; and samadhi, which is the experience of unity with God. The eight limbs are more precisely viewed as eight levels of progress, each level providing benefits in itself and also laying the foundation for the higher levels. The main difference between Raja yoga and Hatha yoga is that Raja yoga uses asanas, or postures, to mainly get the body ready for prolonged meditation and hence focuses more on the meditative asana poses. There are hundreds of asanas, and each asana has particular effects on body and mind.

Karma yoga, or the "discipline of action," is based on the teachings of the Bhagavad-Gita, a sacred Sanskrit scripture of Hinduism. Karma yoga focuses on the adherence to duty (dharma), while remaining detached from the reward. It states that one can attain moksha (salvation) or love of God (bhakti) by performing his or her duties in an unselfish manner for the pleasure of the supreme being. Bhakti yoga denotes the spiritual practice of fostering loving devotion or bhakti to God. Jnana yoga is the yoga of knowledge; jnana meaning knowledge in Sanskrit. .

The importance of breathing is central to all yoga practices. The breath is considered the vehicle of prana, the life force, that enters the body when we inhale. Pranayama, a Sanskrit word meaning lengthening of life force, is vital for all yoga practices. Meditation is another yoga practice; it is a process of focusing the mind into a state of relaxed awareness. Transcendental meditation, introduced in the West in 1960s by Maharishi Mahesh Yogi, transcends normal thought processes to reach a heightened level of cosmic consciousness, producing in the body and mind a profound rest and relaxation. Yoga is the exercise practiced in ayurvedic medicine.

The most important benefit of yoga is physical and mental therapy. The aging process, which is largely an artificial condition caused mainly by autointoxication (self-poisoning), can be slowed down by practicing yoga. By keeping the body clean, flexible, and well lubricated, we can significantly reduce the catabolic process of cell deterioration. To get the maximum benefits of yoga, one has to combine the practices of yogasanas, pranayama, and meditation, which can help diverse ailments, such as diabetes, high blood pressure, digestive disorders, arthritis, arteriosclerosis, chronic fatigue, asthma, varicose veins, and heart conditions. Laboratory tests have proved the yogis' increased ability to consciously control autonomic or involuntary functions, such as temperature, heartbeat, and blood pressure. Research into the effects of yogic practices on HIV is currently underway with promising results. According to medical scientists, yoga therapy is successful because of the balance created in the nervous and endocrine systems, which directly influences all the other systems and organs of the body. Yoga acts both as a curative and preventive therapy. The very essence of yoga lies in attaining mental peace, improved concentration powers, a relaxed state of living, and harmony in relationships. Physicians and scientists continue to discover new health benefits of yoga.

At the core of both yoga and astrology is an understanding of how energy operates in our lives—the energy to express oneself, to establish security, to learn, relate, experience, and love. Yoga understands that energy gains expression through the body, while astrology views the psyche as the central medium. But both disciplines have identified the same basic energies coursing through our lives. Just as yoga strives to achieve oneness between the person's internal constitution and the nature that surrounds it, both ayurveda and astrology strive to equate humans with the factors that surround them.

The planets act like forces that condition the mind and energy patterns in our bodies and minds, keeping them fixed and difficult to change. The discipline that allows mental patterns to be modified, overcoming the stronghold of the planets, is yoga. Hence, yoga not only keeps body and mind healthy, but it also helps alleviate the malefic effects of the planets.

The energies from the Sun and the Moon are manifested in each individual as the two prana poles, or vital energy. They manifest in the process of inhalation and exhalation, as well as in the two main energy channels, or nadis. These nadis are Ida (Moon), located in the left side of the body and connected with the left nostril, and Pingala (Sun), located in the right side of the body and linked with its corresponding nostril. It is from the interaction of these two energies that all mental and physical activity happens. Planetary imbalances on each individual's natal chart produce a disturbance in the energy flow. As one of them is predominant over the other, physical health and mental equilibrium are affected. Through breath control, balance, and regulation of inhalation and exhalation energies, the Hatha yogis are capable of unblocking the nadis; thus, neutralization of the afflictions takes place.

Malefic planetary influences, like the one from Saturn, produce prana blockage and constriction, restricting its flow. Another example is Mars; when afflicted, it generates excitement, restlessness, and prana agitation. These effects can be overcome through the various pranayamas.

Traditional Chinese Medicine and Astrology

Traditional Chinese medicine[45] (also known as TCM) is a range of ancient medical practices that originated in China thousands of years ago. TCM practices include theories, diagnoses, and treatments, such as herbal medicine, acupuncture, and massage. TCM is based on the concept that the human body is a small universe with a set of complete and sophisticated interconnected systems, and that these systems usually work in balance to maintain the healthy function of the human body. The balance of yin and yang is considered with respect to the flow of chi through the meridians, blood, jing ("kidney essence" or "semen"), other bodily fluids, the five elements, emotions, and the shen (soul or spirit). Unlike the Western anatomical model, which divides the physical body into parts, the Chinese model is more concerned with function. Thus, TCM does not treat organs as material things, like heart muscles or glands, but considers them as specific aspects of function associated with physical, emotional, and spiritual properties.

TCM maintains that certain types of imbalances produce one pattern of symptoms in one patient and a different pattern of symptoms in another patient. Hence, TCM physicians examine patients differently from the manner in which Western physicians examine for diagnosis. Four types of examinations help a TCM physician make a diagnosis: visual inspection, voice and body odor, medical history and body complaint, and touches at different parts of the body. TCM also recognizes twenty-eight different pulses in three positions on both wrists for diagnosis.

Much of the scientific research on TCM has focused on acupuncture, which will be discussed later. Much less scientific research has been done on Chinese herbal medicines, which comprise much of TCM. Within China, there has been a great deal of cooperation between TCM practitioners and Western medical doctors . In the West, TCM doctors are not licensed to practice.

TCM deals with the life energy (chi or qi). Chi (pronounced "chee") is the Chinese word used to describe the natural energy of the universe. This energy, though called "natural," is spiritual or supernatural, and is part of a metaphysical belief system. Chi is thought to permeate all things, including the human body. Theories of traditional Chinese medicine assert that the body has natural patterns of chi that circulate in channels called meridians. There are fourteen meridians in human body: central, governing, circulation/sex, bladder, gall bladder, heart, kidney, large intestine, liver, lung, small intestine, spleen, stomach, and triple warmer (glands). Symptoms of various illnesses are often believed to be the product of disrupted, blocked, or unbalanced chi movement through the body's meridians, as well as deficiencies or imbalances of chi in the various organs.

Chi is made up of two dynamic opposites: yang and yin. Yang is considered to be extroverted, excitable, active, light, and male (Sun) energy, whereas yin can be described as introverted, quiet, female, and dark (Moon) energy. Every part of the body has both yang and yin chi aspects to it. Yang conditions are related to dryness and heat, and yin to dampness and cold. If yang and yin are not in balance, the internal organs and other body systems progressively deteriorate and become diseased.

At the cellular level, yang relates to catabolism. If yang is deficient, the body does not clear away weakened cells fast enough. Excessive yang causes the body heat to break down healthy tissues and body ages more quickly. Yang activates the glands, stimulates the adrenals, and turns on testes and ovaries.

Yin cools the body down and affects all body fluids. Deficiency of yin lies at the root of chronic illness and hyperactivity. At the cellular level, yin controls anabolism, the process that builds cells. Too much yin retains fluid causing someone to become overweight. Yin affects the functioning of the immune system, white blood cells, lymph system, and pituitary gland.

Acupuncture

Developed more than five thousand years ago in China, acupuncture is derived from Latin *acus* (needle) and *pungere* (to prick). It is a technique of inserting needles in tiny points on the body for treating illness. In general, hair-thin needles are used in the treatment by acupuncture, but heat, finger pressure, suction, or electrical impulses are also used.

Acupuncture[46] is based on the theory that there are fourteen main energy channels or meridians in our body. Chi flows through these meridians, and each meridian is associated with a particular body function. When the chi flowing through these meridians gets blocked, it causes illness and pain. Each meridian has acupuncture points along its pathway. There are approximately 365 points on the main meridians. Some meridians have more points than the others. The longest meridian, the bladder channel, has sixty-seven points; the shortest meridian, the heart channel, has nine points. When a needle is placed in the acupuncture point, the balance of chi in the patient is restored.

Acupressure is the application of pressure on the acupuncture points with the fingertips. It is not considered as effective as acupuncture. *Shiatsu*, or finger pressure, is a specific type of acupressure developed in Japan. *Moxibustion* stimulates the acupuncture points by burning moxa herb near to the skin. Moxa is made from the leaves of the herb *Artemisia vulgaris. Cupping* uses a cup to stimulate the acupuncture points. Initially, a match is lit under the cup. The burning flame creates a vacuum in the cup, which holds tightly to the skin after the match is removed.

Today acupuncture is practiced by thousands of individuals in many countries in the West like US, Britain, and Canada, not to mention China and other Asian countries. In the West, many of its practitioners have learned in North American and European schools of Eastern medicine. Acupuncture is now being taught in chiropractic and naturopathic medical colleges. An increasing number of M.D.s are learning acupuncture. Acupuncture is now widely used in American hospitals to reduce pain in patients including migraine headache, back pain, and dental pain. It is also being used to treat alcoholism and opiate addiction, and stop smoking.

Scientists are studying the mechanisms and efficacy of acupuncture. Researchers have found good evidence that acupuncture is effective in treating nausea and chronic low back pain, and moderate evidence for effective treatment of neck pain and headache. The World Health Organization (WHO), the National Center for Complementary and Alternative Medicine (NCCAM) of the National Institutes of Health (NIH), the American Medical Association (AMA), and various government organizations have also studied and commented on the efficacy of acupuncture. There is general agreement that acupuncture is safe when administered by well-trained practitioners, and that further research is warranted. Though occasionally charged as pseudoscience, Dr. W. F. Williams, author of *Encyclopedia of Pseudoscience*, notes: *acupuncture—once rejected as "oriental fakery"— is now recognized as something quite real.*

Tai Chi

Tai chi,[47] also known as tai chi ch'uan, is an ancient Chinese exercise that aims at promoting health and longevity. Tai chi translates from Chinese as "supreme ultimate," and tai chi ch'uan means "supreme ultimate boxing or fist." The concept of the "supreme ultimate" is the symbol of the *Taijitu* (Figure 5.1), meant to show the principles of yin and yang duality of Taoist philosophy. Tao means "road" or "path" for living a simple, peaceful life in harmony with the universe. Taoists believe that all elements in the universe are interconnected. This concept is illustrated in the *Taijitu* symbol. The outer circle symbolizes unity. The dark and light areas of the symbol indicate that within unity, there is duality of yang and yin, implying the combination of male/female, light/dark, excitable/quiet, and in/out. The small circles within the dark and light areas represent that there is nothing that is entirely separate from anything else. The center point indicates the balance point for all aspects of life.

Figure 5.1: *Taijitu,* the yin-yang symbol of Taoism

Developed seven hundred years ago, tai chi theory and practice evolved in agreement with many of the principles of Chinese philosophy and Taoism, in particular. Like yoga, tai chi views the mind and body not as separate but as different expressions of life force, or chi. Tai chi training, first and foremost, involves learning solo routines, known as *forms* (*taolu*). While the image of tai chi chuan in popular culture is typified by exceedingly slow movement, many tai chi styles (including the three most popular: yang, wu, and chen) have secondary forms of a faster pace. The other half of traditional tai chi training consists of partner exercises, known as *pushing hands*, and martial applications of the postures of the form.

Along with yoga, tai chi is one of the fastest growing fitness and health-maintenance activities in the West. Studies have indicated that tai chi improves cardiovascular and respiratory function in healthy subjects, as well as those who have undergone coronary artery bypass surgery. Patients who suffer from heart failure, high blood pressure, heart attacks, arthritis, multiple sclerosis, Parkinson's, and Alzheimer's may also benefit from tai chi.

Chinese Astrology and TCM

Five elements in Chinese philosophy are different from the Western and Indian elements. The five Chinese elements are metal, wood, water, fire, and earth. The ancient Chinese astronomers called the five major planets by the names of the elements with which they were associated:

- Venus: metal

- Jupiter: wood

- Mercury: water

- Mars: fire

- Saturn: earth

The Zodiacs in Chinese astrology have a twelve-year cycle.

Each year of the twelve-year cycle is named after one of the original twelve animals. Each animal has a different personality and different characteristics. The animal is believed to be the main factor in each person's life, which gives him his traits, success, and happiness in his lifetime. The twelve Zodiacs are as follows: rat, ox, tiger, rabbit, dragon, snake, horse, sheep, monkey, rooster, dog, and pig. The system of the twelve-year cycle of animal signs was built from observations of the orbit of Jupiter, which goes round the Sun once in 11.86 years. Following the orbit of Jupiter around the Sun, Chinese astronomers divided the celestial circle into twelve sections, and rounded it to twelve years (from 11.86 years).

However, since the traditional Chinese Zodiac follows the lunisolar Chinese calendar, the switchover date is the Chinese New Year, not January 1, as in the Gregorian calendar. In the Gregorian calendar, Chinese New Year falls on different dates each year, a date between January 21 and February 20.

It is a common misconception that the animals assigned by year are the only signs, and many Western descriptions of Chinese astrology draw solely on this system. In fact, there are also animal signs assigned by month (called inner animals) and hours of the day (called secret animals). Therefore, while a person might appear to be a dragon because he was born in the year of the dragon, he might also be a snake internally and an ox secretively. In total, this makes for 8,640 possible combinations: five elements multiplied by the twelve animals in the sixty-year cycle (5 x 12 = 60), twelve months, twelve times of day. These are all considered critical for the proper use of Chinese astrology.

The attributes of the Chinese elements are given in Table 5.2.

Table 5.2: Attributes of Chinese elements

Chinese Element	Season	Color	Yang organ	Yin organ	Orifice
Wood	Spring	Green	Gall bladder	Liver	Eyes
Metal	Autumn	White	Large intestine	Lung	Mouth
Fire	Summer	Red	Small intestine	Heart	Ears
Water	Winter	Black	Bladder	Kidney	Urinary
Earth	Indian summer	Yellow	Stomach	Spleen	Nose

Traditional Chinese medicine has twelve regular meridians. Ten of them are associated with actual organs. If we take these regular meridians and then apply the Western planetary rules, we can create a bridge between the Chinese astrology and Western astrology, as shown in Table 5.3.

Table 5.3: Relationship between Chinese astrology
and Western astrology

Chinese Meridian	Western Planetary Ruler
Heart (yin/fire)	Sun
Small intestine (yang/fire)	Mercury/Moon
Lung (yin/metal)	Jupiter
Large intestine (yang/metal)	Mercury/Moon
Spleen (yin/earth)	Saturn
Stomach (yang/earth)	Moon
Liver (yin/wood)	Jupiter
Gall bladder (yang/wood)	Mars
Kidney (yin/water)	Venus
Urinary bladder (yang/water)	Moon/Saturn
Pericardium (yin/water)	None
Triple warmer** (yang/fire)	None

** In TCM, triple warmer is the texture beneath skin and between muscles. There have been some proposed theories stating that this conceptual organ corresponds to the lymphatic system.

From an astrological perspective, we can use the chart to diagnose the organs affected and use TCM to bolster these organs through acupuncture, acupressure, moxibustion, or use of herbs. We can also use the natal chart to identify which organs are more likely to develop diseases, so that the individuals can use these as an early warning system for possible health setbacks.

Feng Shui

The words *feng shui* literally translate as "wind water." Feng shui is an ancient Chinese practice believed to utilize the laws of both heaven and earth to help one improve life by receiving positive chi. Feng shui is the practice of arranging objects (such as furniture) to help people achieve their goals. More traditionally, feng shui is important in choosing a place to live and finding a burial site, along with agricultural planning. Proponents claim that feng shui has an effect on health, wealth, and personal relationships.

The goal of feng shui, as practiced today, is to situate the human-built environment on locations with good chi. The "perfect spot" is a location and an axis in time. Some areas are not suitable for human settlement and should be left in their natural state. Feng shui uses a holistic understanding of local microclimates (local atmospheric zones where the climate differs from the surrounding area), the orientation of the structure, its age, and its interaction with the surrounding environment, from the slope of the land to the vegetation and soil quality.

In feng shui, a house is divided into nine grids, within which there are eight sectors, or directions: the center, four primary sectors, and four secondary sectors. The four primary sectors are north, south, east and west, whereas the four secondary sectors are northwest, southeast, northeast, and southwest. The center of a house is not included in the compass directions. The animal sign that rules the year is given the peculiar name of Grand Duke Jupiter, which is associated with the celestial bodies. Every year, the Grand Duke Jupiter will move into a different sector in the house, and the place it occupies for the year will be afflicted with negative energies. These negative energies will afflict the resident who resides in the sector concerned. This affliction will manifest in unlucky outcomes for the resident, such as accidents, financial losses, and illnesses. Appropriate arrangements, according to feng shui, should be made to vitiate the malefic effect of the Grand Duke Jupiter, thus exemplifying how Chinese astrology and feng shui complement each other.

Concluding Remarks

The human body is not made just of molecules and cells; there is also a life form that keeps the body alive and functioning. This life force has been explained as prana, chi, and other names in ancient cultures. All alternative medicine, practiced from ancient times until now, is based on balancing this life force. Astrology studies the relationships between the planets and celestial objects and the life force. Practitioners of the alternative medicine consult the birth charts of their patients to diagnose their illnesses. This joint effort should be more encouraged and practiced. Although scientists may denounce these practices, they cannot deny the effectiveness of these treatments. Treatments are not necessarily invalid simply because they cannot be explained by current scientific theory.

Natural forces within us are the true healers of disease.

—Hippocrates

Chapter 6
Astrology is Explained by Cosmic Energy and Biofield

It is clearly evident that most events of a widespread nature draw their causes from the enveloping heavens.

—Claudius Ptolemy

In this chapter, I will discuss the fourth good reason why astrology is a science: astrology is explained by cosmic energy and biofield. I will first describe the source of cosmic energy that reaches Earth—the celestial bodies of the universe. These celestial bodies are the stars, including our own Sun. These stars produce cosmic energy when they explode as nova or supernova. The Sun also produces solar wind of cosmic particles that reach Earth. I will then describe the human biofield and how the cosmic particles that reach Earth could affect the biofield, with an effect on our bodies and behavior. The word "universe" is derived from the Old Greek *univers* and from Latin *universa*, which combines *uni* ("one") with *versus* ("turn"). The word, therefore, means "all turned into one," or "revolving as one," or "orbiting as one."

The size of the universe is estimated to be seventy-eight billion light-years, expanding at the rate of 138 miles per second for every ten million light-years. There are approximately one hundred billion galaxies, including our own Milky Way, in the universe. An important question is the shape of the universe. Most cosmologists believe that the universe is nearly spatially flat.

Origin of the Universe

The universe originated from a Big Bang.[48] Approximately 13.7 billion years ago, our universe was compressed into confines of an atomic nucleus, known as singularity. This was the moment before creation when space and time did not exist. Then an indescribable explosion, trillions of degrees in temperature, created not only fundamental subatomic particles and radiation energy but also space and time. This explosion is called the Big Bang.

Observational evidence for the Big Bang comes from the redshift of the spectra of galaxies proportional to their distance as described by Hubble's law. Redshift is basically the Doppler effect applied to light waves. Doppler effect states that the frequency from a light wave of a moving object decreases as it moves away from us. Stars have sets of absorption and emission lines identifiable in their spectra. If a star is moving toward us, its light waves get crowded together, raising the frequency. Because the blue light is at the high-frequency end of the visible spectrum, this is known as blueshift. If the star is receding, the spectrum lines move towards the red end and the effect is known as redshift.

American astronomer Edwin Hubble (1889–1953) discovered a proportionality of the distance of the stars with their redshift. Hubble and American astronomer Milton Humason were able to plot a trend line from the forty-six galaxies they studied and proposed Hubble's law,[49] which states that the radial velocity, v, with which a galaxy recedes is linearly proportional to its distance, r, from us.

$$v \propto r ; \quad v = H.r ; \text{ where, } H = \text{Hubble constant.}$$

The current estimate of Hubble constant H from measurements using the Hubble Space Telescope is $H = 72$ Km per second per megaparsec (1 parsec = 3.261 light years = 19.174 x 10^{12} miles; 1 megaparsec = 19.174 x 10^{18} miles).

Now, the distance *r* is given by the velocity *v* multiplied by time *t*. as follows:

$$r = v.t = v \,/\, H.$$

Hence, $t = 1 \,/\, H$. Substituting the value of *H*, $t = 1 \,/\, (72$ x sec^{-1} x 3.3 x 10^{-20}) = 13.3 billion years, which is very close to the estimated age of the universe.

The next most important observational evidence was the discovery of cosmic microwave background radiation in 1964. This was predicted as a relic from the time when hot ionized plasma of the early universe first cooled sufficiently to form neutral hydrogen and allowed space to become transparent to light. Its discovery led to the general acceptance among physicists that the Big Bang was the best model for the origin and evolution of the universe. Another important line of evidence is the relative proportion of light elements in the universe, which is a close match to the predictions for the formation of light elements in the first minutes of the universe, according to the Big Bang theory.

The next question that comes up is "Where did the Big Bang happen?" The answer is that it happened everywhere. In cosmological principle, no point in the universe is special. Also, space and time were created at the instant of Big Bang. Thus, any point now would trace back to the point of the Big Bang. In that respect, Big Bang happened everywhere in space.

Approximately 10^{-35} seconds into the expansion, a phase transition caused a cosmic inflation, during which the universe grew exponentially. The universe was filled homogeneously and isotropically with an incredibly high energy density, huge temperatures, and pressures and was very rapidly expanding and cooling. After inflation stopped, the universe consisted of a quark-gluon plasma, as well as all other elementary particles like quarks, leptons, and bosons. The nucleus of an atom consists of protons and neutrons. A protons has a positive charge, while a neutron has no charge. Protons and neutrons are made of quarks bonded by gluons.

Leptons are electron, muon, and tau with negative charge. A muon is two hundred times heavier than an electron; a tau is heavier than a muon. Temperatures during this period were so high that the random motions of particles were at a significant fraction of the speed of light, and particle-antiparticle pairs of all kinds were being continuously created and destroyed in collisions.

The universe continued to grow in size and fall in temperature; hence, the typical energy of each particle was decreasing. After about 10^{-11} seconds, the picture became less speculative, since particle energies dropped to values that can be attained in particle physics experiments. The temperature was about 10^{15} K, and free electrons, quarks, photons, and neutrinos were strongly interacting with each other. One second after the initial explosion, the temperature dropped to 10^{10} K, photons no longer had the energy to disrupt the creation of nucleus consisting of neutron and proton, and nucleosynthesis began to form nucleus of an atom.

The universe was still radiation dominated. At 10^{13} seconds after the initial explosion, when the universe was 300,000 years old, the temperature dropped to 3,000 K, atoms formed from nuclei and electrons. The photons were no longer interacting with them, and were cooling to form what is known as the microwave background. This process is known as decoupling. The decoupling happened when the universe was one-thousandth of its present size.

In the early universe, the only elements produced in any significant abundance were hydrogen and helium-4 (nucleus with 2 protons and 2 neutrons). Helium-4 was produced since it has the most stable light nucleus, and hydrogen was produced because there were not enough neutrons around for all protons to bind with and so some protons were left over.

After decoupling, clouds of gas and dust, called nebulae, began to form, which were constantly in motion. As a result, some regions in the nebulae periodically had a higher concentration of gas and dust than others, causing stronger force of gravity in those regions. When the force of gravity was sufficiently strong in a particular region, a star was formed. As the collection of gas and dust in the star continued, temperature at the center rose higher and higher. When the temperature reached 18 million°F, nuclear fusion took place, and a star was born.

Many stars are between one billion and ten billion years old. Some stars may even be close to 13.7 billion years old—the observed age of the universe. The more massive the star, the shorter its lifespan, primarily because massive stars have greater pressure on their cores, causing them to burn hydrogen more rapidly. The most massive stars last an average of about one million years, while stars of minimum mass (red dwarfs) burn their fuel very slowly and last tens to hundreds of billions of years.

Galaxies

Stars form the galaxies. A galaxy (from the Greek term *galaxias*, meaning "milky," a reference to our own Milky Way) is a massive, gravitationally bound system consisting of stars, an interstellar medium of gas and dust, and dark matter. Typical galaxies range from dwarfs with as few as ten million stars up to giants with one trillion stars, all orbiting a common center of mass. Galaxies can also contain many multiple star systems, star clusters, and various interstellar clouds. A common form is the elliptical galaxy, which has an ellipse-shaped light profile. Spiral galaxies are disk-shaped assemblages with curving, dusty arms. Galaxies with irregular or unusual shapes are known as peculiar galaxies and typically result from disruption by the gravitational pull of neighboring galaxies.

Most galaxies are 1,000 to 100,000 parsecs in diameter and are usually separated by distances on the order of millions of parsecs (or megaparsecs). Intergalactic space (the space between galaxies) is filled with a tenuous gas of an average density less than one atom per cubic meter. The majority of galaxies are organized into a hierarchy of associations called clusters, which, in turn, can form larger groups called superclusters. Although it is not yet well understood, dark matter appears to account for around 90% of the mass of most galaxies. Observational data suggests that supermassive black holes may exist at the center of many, if not all, galaxies. They are proposed to be the primary cause of active galactic nuclei found at the core of some galaxies. The Milky Way galaxy, home of Earth and the solar system, appears to harbor at least one such black hole within its nucleus.

The Milky Way galaxy is the home of our solar system, together with at least 200 billion other stars (more recent estimates have given numbers around 400 billion) and their planets, and thousands of clusters and nebulae. All the objects in the Milky Way galaxy orbit their common center of mass, called the galactic center. As a galaxy, the Milky Way is actually a giant, as its mass is probably between 750 billion and one trillion solar masses.

Our star Sun, together with the whole solar system, is orbiting the galactic center on a nearly circular orbit. We are moving at about 156 miles/second and need about 220 million years to complete one orbit. So the solar system has orbited the galactic center about twenty or twenty-one times since its formation about 4.6 billion years ago.

The Milky Way consists of the flowing areas:

1. The galactic center and bulge around the center.

2. The disk with spiral arms, which contains the majority of the stars, including the Sun, and virtually all of the gas and dust.

3. The halo, a roughly spherical distribution, which contains the oldest stars in the galaxy

The galactic center harbors a compact object of very large mass (named Sagittarius A), strongly suspected to be a supermassive black hole. Most galaxies are believed to have a supermassive black hole at their center. The bulge is composed primarily of red stars and molecular hydrogen gas.

The galactic disk has a diameter of between 70,000 and 100,000 light-years. The disc is believed to have four major spiral arms, which all start at the galaxy's center. The Sun is located in one of the spiral arm about two-thirds of the way from the center to the edge of the disk (about 25,000 light-years, by the most modern estimates).

The galactic disk is surrounded by a spheroid halo of old stars and globular clusters, with a stellar halo diameter of 200,000 light-years.

However, a few globular clusters have been found farther away, at more than 200,000 light-years away from the galactic center.

Sun

Because of the Sun's enormous bulk and mass, the pressure at the center is extremely high, as is the density (150 times the density of water on Earth), and the temperature (around 15 million degrees). Under these conditions, the atoms are moving about so rapidly and colliding with one another so violently that they split into their component particles: protons, alpha particles, and electrons. In the Sun's core, four protons are forced into one alpha particle (a nucleus of a helium 4 atom), and in this process, which is called nuclear fusion, a small mass from these particles is converted into energy. The core of the Sun is, therefore, similar to a vast thermonuclear furnace, in which billions and billions of these particles are continually being fused, with the result that 4 million tons of solar materials are converted into energy each second. This energy radiates outward from the core, and it is then transported through the Sun's outer layer to the surface.

The Sun maintains its stable equilibrium under the opposing action of two gigantic forces: the gravitational force pulling inward and the pressure of gas pushing outward; these exactly balance each other. The Sun has been shining for 4.6 billion years and has so far converted about one hundred Earth masses into energy. At this rate, it has enough energy to last another 5 billion years.

As a star burns out, it ends up as a red giant, white dwarf, nova, or super nova.

Red Giant

A red giant is a luminous giant star of low or intermediate mass that is in a later phase of its evolution, with nuclear fusion going on in a shell outside the core but not in the core itself. Red giants evolve from main sequence stars, with masses in the range from about 0.5 solar masses to somewhere between 4 and 6 solar masses. After a few billion years, the center of a star runs out of hydrogen. What is left is a central region of helium. The outer layers of the star still contain hydrogen, but it is not hot enough to fuse. Because the star has run out of fuel, it begins to cool. The outer layers of the star fall inward due to gravity, and as they fall, they heat up. A shell surrounding the central core becomes hot enough to fuse hydrogen into helium. So the star gains a new source of energy. The core of the star is now hotter than it was during its normal life. The heat generated from this energy causes the outer layers of the star to expand greatly. Due to the expansion of the outer layers, the energy is spread over a larger surface area, resulting a in a lower surface temperature and shift in the star's visible light output toward red—hence, the red giant, although the color is usually orange.

The Sun is expected to become a red giant in about 5.5 billion years. It is calculated that the sun will become almost sufficiently large to engulf the current orbits of some of the solar system's inner planets, including Earth. However, the gravitational pull of the Sun will have weakened by then, due to its loss of mass, and all planets but Mercury will escape to a wider orbit.

White Dwarf

Although the outer layer of the red giant gets cooler, its core temperature increases until it is hot enough to transform helium, created from hydrogen fusion, into carbon and other heavier elements. When the red giant has finished its helium, it is not hot enough to burn the carbon it created, so it succumbs to gravity again. When the core of the red giant contracts, it causes a release of energy that makes it envelop to expand, making it an even bigger giant than before. It becomes unstable and blows off its outer layer. The core remains intact and becomes a white dwarf. A white dwarf is very dense, as its mass is comparable to the Sun's and its volume is comparable to Earth's. Our Sun will ultimately become a white dwarf.

Nova

When a white dwarf is close to a companion star, the white dwarf will accrete hydrogen from the atmosphere of the companion star. The companion star could be another star or a red giant. Hydrogen becomes enormously compressed by the white dwarf's strong force of gravity to the point of detonation. At this moment, the outer layer of the white dwarf is turned into a giant hydrogen bomb. The enormous amount of energy liberated by this process blows away the remaining gases from the white dwarf's surface and produces an extremely bright outburst of light. This event is called nova.

Supernova

Supernova is a giant nova. It may be created in two ways. One possible cause is the collapse of a massive star. After the core of an aging massive star ceases to generate energy from nuclear fusion, it may undergo sudden gravitational collapse into a neutron star or black hole, releasing gravitational potential energy that heats and expels the star's outer layers. Another possible cause is that a white dwarf may accumulate sufficient material from a stellar companion to raise its core temperature enough to ignite carbon fusion, at which point it undergoes runaway nuclear fusion, completely disrupting it. Supernova occurs about once every fifty years in a galaxy such as our Milky Way. The earliest recorded supernova, SN 185, was viewed by Chinese astronomers in CE 185. The widely observed supernova of SN 1054 in the year 1054 produced the Crab Nebula in the Milky Way

Neutron Star and Pulsar

When a supernova detonates, its core continues to collapse by its own gravity, past the white dwarf stage, past the point where the star would be held by the repulsive force of its own electrons, until its electrons and protons are squeezed together in to neutrons. The entire star becomes a ball of neutrons less than ten miles across and is called a neutron star. While a teaspoonful of a white dwarf, if brought to Earth, would weigh a couple of tons, a teaspoonful of a neutron star would weigh over 500 million tons.

The neutron star would spin at the rate of about twelve times a second. Its magnetic field also increases dramatically. It traps charged particles from the atmosphere and forces them to spiral frantically about at nearly the speed of light, as they are dragged around with the spinning star. In so doing, the particles emit two narrow beams that shoot out from opposite points on the star, causing the star to appear like giant cosmic lighthouse. Neutron stars that appear to pulse in this way are called pulsars. The Crab Nebula has a pulsar.

Black Hole

If a supernova leaves behind a core that has a mass more than three times the mass of the Sun, it becomes a black hole. It has such a strong gravitational force that not even light can escape. Hence, it is called a black hole. Supermassive black holes that contain millions to billion times the mass of the Sun are believed to exist in the center of most galaxies.

Quasar

A quasar, derived from the words "quasi-stellar radio source," is an extremely bright and active galactic nucleus. A quasar is a compact halo of matter surrounding the central, supermassive black hole of a young galaxy. Quasars are believed to be powered by accretion of material into supermassive black holes in the nuclei of distant galaxies. Quasars are the brightest objects in the universe.

Composition of the Universe

The most recent Wilkinson Microwave Anisotropy Probe (WMAP) observations predict that the universe is made of 74% dark energy, 22% dark matter, and 4% baryonic matter[50] (hydrogen, helium, stars, neutrinos, and others), as shown in Figure 6.1. It has been found that the mass of the baryonic matter in the galaxies is not enough to explain the rotation of the galaxies. The centrifugal acceleration and the gravitational pull, due to mass in the galaxy, must balance out for the galaxy to be stable. The visible part of the galaxy that contains the baryonic matters is within radius *R*. The mass outside the radius *R* does not contribute to the gravitational pull.

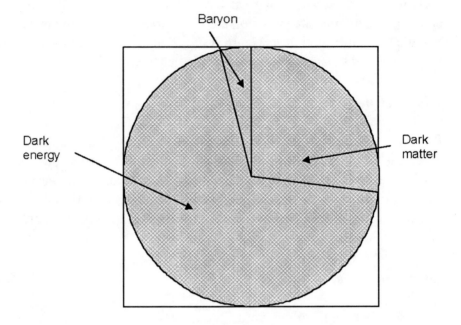

Figure 6.1: Composition of universe

Hence, the rotational velocity should drop off as the square root of radius *R*. Instead, it is found more or less constant. This is due to dark matter, which is nonbaryonic and interacts extremely weakly with conventional matter.

Dark energy solves the missing mass problem of the universe. For the universe to be flat, the mass/energy density of the universe must be equal to a certain critical density, 10^{-26} Kg m^{-3}. The total amount of matter in the universe (including baryons and dark matter) accounts for only about 30 percent of the critical density. This implies the existence of an additional form of energy to account for the remaining 70 percent, called dark energy.

During the late 1990s, measurements of type 1A supernovae by the Supernova Cosmology Project and High-Z Supernova Search Team in the United States suggested that that the expansion of the universe is accelerating. These observations are explained by postulating that dark energy has negative pressure.

The exact nature of this dark energy is a matter of speculation. It is known to be very homogeneous, not very dense, and is not known to interact through any of the fundamental forces, other than gravity. Because it is not very dense—roughly 10^{-29} grams per cubic centimeter—it is difficult to find of experiments that will detect it in the laboratory.

Cosmic Energy

When a nova or supernova explodes, it discharges vast amount of cosmic rays. These cosmic rays are protons of the elements in the periodic table. The dominant elements are hydrogen and helium, along with other light elements (lithium, beryllium, and boron), with a few others, such as carbon and oxygen. However, these cosmic rays reaching Earth are deflected by the electromagnetic field present throughout the galaxy, including the field of the Sun and planets and their satellites in the solar system. When these cosmic rays reach Earth, they collide with the atoms of the upper atmosphere of Earth, releasing showers of gamma rays, x-rays, and subatomic particles.

Solar activity in the Sun also produces cosmic rays. Sunspots appear on the Sun's visible surface from time to time. A sunspot consists of a dark central region (umbra) surrounded by a lighter gray area (penumbra). The largest spots are far larger than Earth and are often irregular in shape. Because of the Sun's irregular rotation, it is possible to observe sunspots drifting across the Sun's face from day to day at different speeds, according to their solar latitude. The lifetime of sunspots is between a few hours and many weeks. The sunspots are a relatively cooler region in the photosphere, about 2000° K, than the surrounding area, which explains their dark color. Sunspots are localized areas of a powerful magnetic field. The number of sunspots increases or decreases in an eleven-year cycle, with a maxima in 1958, 1969, 1980,1991, and 2002.

Other solar activities include prominences, plages, and flares. Prominences are visible eclipse of the Sun and are clouds of hot gas, some of which surge violently upwards, occasionally to more than 100,000 miles above the photosphere. Plages are masses of incandescent gas in the chromosphere and are heated by strong magnetic fields.

A solar flare is a sudden local explosion occurring in a particular region of the Sun's atmosphere, caused by powerful local magnetic field. Flares cause violent shock waves to travel through the Sun's surface at more than 1000 miles per hour, and they release an intense burst of energy in the form of x-rays, ultraviolet rays, radio waves, and energetic charged particles.

As the solar activity increases, a constant stream of electrically charged particles is radiated in all directions from the Sun. This is known as the solar wind, with a million tons of solar-wind material leaving the Sun's vicinity every second. Solar flares add particles to the solar-wind material, resulting in sudden surges.

A constant stream of electrons from the Sun is responsible for the "auroras" on Earth. The solar wind caused by a solar flare contains a million tons of electrically charged subatomic particles that leave the Sun every second, disturbing Earth's magnetic field, as well as that of other planets, forming a magnetosphere for each planet.

The space surrounding the Sun, its corona and beyond, is a plasma. Each planet has a plasma sheath; the size of which is determined by the difference between the electrical potential of the planet and that of the nearby solar plasma. The shape of this plasma sheath is usually a teardrop, the pointed end facing away from the Sun. The plasma sheath of Venus is extremely long, almost touching Earth when the two planets are at their closest approach. There are strong "dust devils"[51] on Mars, which is a dust storm of highly charged particles.

Sun's Magnetic Field

The differential rotation of the Sun's latitudes causes its magnetic field lines to become twisted together over time, causing magnetic field loops to erupt from the Sun's surface and triggering the formation of the Sun's dramatic sunspots. This twisting action gives rise to a solar cycle of magnetic activity, as the Sun's magnetic field reverses itself about every eleven years.

The interplanetary magnetic field (IMF), as shown in Figure

6.2, is a part of the Sun's magnetic field that is carried into the interplanetary space by the solar wind. Because of the Sun's rotation, the IMF, like the solar wind, travels outward in a spiral pattern that is often compared to the pattern of water sprayed from a lawn sprinkler. The IMF originates in regions on the Sun where the magnetic field is open; that is. where the field lines

Interplanetary
current sheet

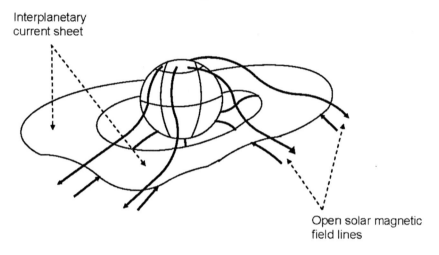

Open solar magnetic
field lines

Figure 6.2: Interplanetary magnetic field (IMF)

emerging from one region do not return to a conjugate region but extend virtually indefinitely into space. The direction of the field in the Sun's Northern Hemisphere is opposite to that of the field in the Southern Hemisphere, with the polarities reversing with each solar cycle.

The oppositely directed open magnetic-field lines along the plane of the Sun's magnetic equator run parallel to each other and are separated by a thin current sheet known as the heliospheric current sheet[52]. The current sheet is tilted because of an offset between the Sun's rotational and magnetic axes. The current sheet is also warped because of the change in the polarity of the spiraling magnetic field. Thus, the heliospheric current sheet has a wavy ballerina-skirt–like structure as it extends in to IMF. Because Earth is located sometimes above and some times below the heliospheric current sheet, it experiences regular, periodic changes in the polarity of the IMF.

Flow of Cosmic Particles in the Solar System

How do cosmic particles flowing in the solar system reach Earth? The solar magnetic field reverses at each maximum solar activity, resulting in a twenty-two years cycle. The field orientation is known as its polarity; it is positive when the field is outward from the Sun in the Northern Hemisphere and is negative when the field is outward in the Southern Hemisphere. The intensity of the galactic cosmic rays varies inversely with the sunspot number, as shown in Figure 6.3. Cosmic rays have their maximum intensity at the minimum spot cycle. Hence, the energy particles that reach Earth originates alternately from two sources—galactic energy particles during minimum sunspot cycles, and solar energy particles during maximum sunspot cycles. During each cycle, the positions of the planets affect the flow of energy particles to Earth.

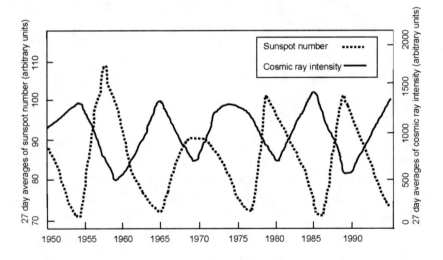

Figure 6.3: Sunspot number *(dotted line)* and the cosmic ray intensity *(solid line)*

Remember that the reversing solar magnetic field gives rise to the interplanetary magnetic field (IMF) and heliospheric current sheet (HCS). The current sheet is tilted and is not flat but wavy, like a ballerina's skirt, rotating with the Sun every twenty-seven days. At solar minimum, the waviness of the HCS is limited to about 10 degrees helio-latitude, but near solar maximum, the extent of the HCS may almost reach the poles. With the rotation of the HCS every twenty-seven days, Earth is alternately above and below the sheet, and thus in an alternating magnetic field directed toward or away from the Sun.

Due to the gradient of the magnetic field around the HCS and the reversal of the direction of the magnetic field from one side of the HCS to the other side, the cosmic ray particles experience an effective drift along the HCS. The direction of the drift depends on the polarity of the solar magnetic field, which changes every eleven years. During the period when the magnetic field is outward from the Sun in the Northern Hemisphere (state A), the cosmic ray particles enter the heliosphere along the polar axis and rarely encounter the HCS on their inward journey, as shown in Figure 6.4 (case 1). This was the period

Case 1: Solar magnetic field outward from the Sun in the northern hemisphere

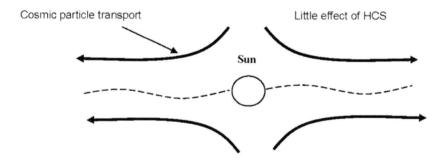

Case 2: Solar magnetic field outward from the Sun in the southern hemisphere

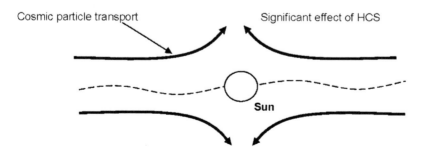

Figure 6.4: Galactic cosmic ray transport

during the 1970s and 1990s. During the period when the magnetic field was outward from the Sun in the Southern Hemisphere (state B) during 1980s and 2000s, the cosmic particles entered the heliosphere along the heliographic equator and would interact with the HCS, resulting in a radial drift along the HCS towards the Sun, as shown in Figure 6.4 (case 2). The transport of cosmic rays would result in a minimum cosmic-ray density at the HCS during state A and a maximum at the HCS during state B.

Planets Affecting the Solar Wind That Reaches Earth

Charged particles from the solar wind cannot reach Earth's atmosphere directly; they are deflected by Earth's magnetosphere and aggregate to form the Van Allen radiation belts. The Van Allen belts consist of an inner belt, composed primarily of protons, and an outer belt, composed mostly of electrons. The Van Allen belts form arcs around Earth, with their tips near the North and South Poles. The most energetic particles can leak out of the belts and strike Earth's upper atmosphere, causing auroras, known as the aurora borealis in the Northern Hemisphere and the aurora australis in the Southern Hemisphere.

The planets that affect the flow of solar wind that reaches Earth are Mercury and Venus, placed between Earth and the Sun[53] (Figure 6.5A). The tail of the magnetosphere of Venus almost touches Earth when the two planets are at their closest approach. The weak magnetic moment of Mercury, combined with a solar-wind pressure about seven times larger than the pressure at Earth, results in a very small planetary magnetosphere (in both absolute dimensions and relative to the size of the planet). The magnetic cavity deflects the solar wind at a distance of only 1.5 Mercury radii from the center of the planet. Very little is known, however, about the Mercury magnetosphere.

Planets Affecting the Cosmic Energies That Reach Earth

Cosmic energies are generated by the supernovae in the galaxies and are protons of mainly hydrogen and helium. During the period when the magnetic field is outward from the Sun in the Northern Hemisphere (case 1), these cosmic rays enter the solar system or heliosphere along the polar axis, as shown in Figure 6.5a. During the period when the magnetic field is outward from the Sun in the Southern Hemisphere, the cosmic particles interact with the HCS, resulting in a radial drift along the HCS toward the Sun,[53] as shown in Figure 6.5b.

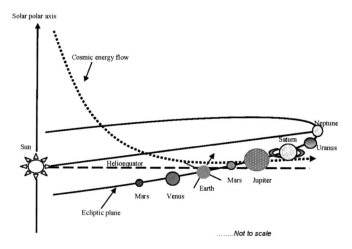

Figure 6.5a: Cosmic energy flow when the solar magnetic flow is outward from the Sun in the Northern Hemisphere

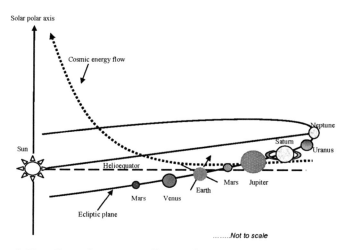

Figure 6.5b: Cosmic energy flow when the solar magnetic field is outward from the Sun in the Southern Hemisphere

In case 1, because all planets are on the ecliptic plane, there are no planets located on the polar axis of the Sun. Only Mercury and Venus may affect the flow of cosmic energies that reach Earth, as they may lie in the exit path of the flow along the equator. But because the magnetic field of Mercury and Venus is very low, there is very little impact on the flow by these two planets.

In case 2, the cosmic energies that reach Earth are affected by outer planets (i.e., Mars, Jupiter, Saturn, Uranus, Neptune, and Pluto), when they are in conjunction with Earth (i.e., placed on the line connecting Earth to the Sun). The planets with an appreciable magnetic field affect the cosmic rays. Hence, Jupiter will have the strongest impact, followed by Saturn, Uranus, and Neptune. Mars and Pluto have virtually no effect, due to an absence of an intrinsic magnetic field (Table 6.1). However, there are strong "dust devils" on Mars—dust storms of highly charged particles. These energy particles reach Earth due to the close proximity of Mars to Earth.

The Moon has virtually no magnetic field and no atmosphere. Hence, the cosmic rays and solar rays directly hit the Moon. The Moon is at an average distance of 238,800 miles from Earth, its main effect on the cosmic particles and solar rays is due to shielding.

Cyclic Pattern of Cosmic Energies and Solar Wind Affecting Earth

Cosmic energies and solar flares are dominant in alternate periods of an eleven-year solar cycle. During first 5.5-year period of the solar cycle, the solar flares are maximum, and the cosmic energies are minimum. During the second 5.5-year period, the solar flares are minimum, and the cosmic energies are maximum. There is another phenomenon associated with this and that is the solar magnetic cycle. The magnetic polarity of the Sun reverses at each maximum solar flare cycle, resulting in a twenty-two–year solar magnetic cycle. Hence in a twenty-two–year solar magnetic cycle, there are two 5.5-year periods of dominant solar flares and two 5.5-year periods of dominant cosmic energies. During a one-half period of the solar magnetic cycle, lasting eleven years, the solar magnetic field is of positive polarity, with the magnetic field going outward in the

Northern Hemisphere, and there is one 5.5-year period of dominant solar flares and one 5.5-year period of dominant cosmic energies. During the other one-half period of the solar magnetic cycle, the solar magnetic field is of negative polarity, with the magnetic field going outward in the Southern Hemisphere and similarly including one 5.5-year period of dominant solar flares and one 5.5-year period of dominant cosmic energies.

The effect of the planets on the cosmic energies and solar flares is shown in Table 6.1. During the period of maximum solar flares, Mercury and Venus affect the flow of solar energies reaching Earth, as the magnetospheres of these two planets are in the path of the solar plasma between the Sun and Earth. During the period of maximum cosmic energies when the solar magnetic field is outward from the Sun in the Northern Hemisphere, because the planets lie in the ecliptic plane and not on the polar axis of the Sun, only Mercury and Venus may affect the cosmic energy flow, as shown in Figure 6.6a. But because the magnetic field of Mercury and Venus is almost zero, they have minor effect on the cosmic energy flow. Again, during the period of maximum cosmic energies when the solar magnetic field is outward from the Sun in the Southern Hemisphere, the following planets lying along the ecliptic plane (conjunction with Earth) affect the flow of cosmic energies reaching Earth—Jupiter, Saturn, Uranus, and Neptune, as shown in Figure 6.5b.

Table 6.1: Effect of planets on cosmic energies
and solar flares reaching

Solar magnetic cycle	Solar magnetic field outward from the Sun in the Northern Hemisphere	Solar magnetic field outward from the Sun in the Northern Hemisphere	Solar magnetic field outward from the Sun in the Southern Hemisphere	Solar magnetic field outward from the Sun in the Southern Hemisphere
Solar flares	Maximum	Minimum	Maximum	Minimum
Cosmic energies	Minimum	Maximum	Minimum	Maximum
Flow of cosmic energies		Enters along the polar axis of the heliosphere		Enters along the helioequator of the heliosphere
Planets affecting cosmic energies and solar flares reaching Earth	Mercury and Venus in conjunction with Earth	Mercury and Venus with minor impact due to very low intrinsic magnetic field	Mercury and Venus in conjunction with Earth	Jupiter, Saturn, Uranus, and Neptune in conjunction with Earth

Summary of the Flow of Cosmic Particles Reaching Earth

The following summary is drawn from the discussions above:

1. Energy particles reach Earth from solar flares during a sunspot cycle and from galaxies as cosmic energy particles.

2. Cosmic energies and solar flares occur alternately each with a period of 5.5 years.

3. Solar magnetic field reverses every eleven years with a cycle period of twenty-two years. In this solar magnetic cycle, there two 5.5-year periods of solar flares and two 5.5-year periods of cosmic energies.

4. When the solar magnetic field is outward from the Sun in the Northern Hemisphere, the cosmic energies enter along

the polar axis of the heliosphere, travel down, and exit along the helioequator.

5. When the solar magnetic field is outward from the Sun in the Southern Hemisphere, the cosmic energies enter along the helioequator of the heliosphere, and exit along the polar axis.

6. During the period of the solar flares, Mercury and Venus have an effect on the solar energy particles reaching Earth, when they are in conjunction with Earth.

7. During the period of cosmic energies, when the solar magnetic field is outward from the Sun in the Northern Hemisphere, Mercury and Venus may have minor effect on the cosmic energies reaching Earth.

8. During the period of cosmic energies, when the solar magnetic field is outward from the Sun in the Southern Hemisphere, Jupiter, Saturn, Uranus, and Neptune will affect the flow of cosmic energies reaching Earth when they are in conjunction with Earth.

9. Other phenomena of the planets, such as dust devils on Mars, may send energy particles to Earth.

10. The Moon may affect the solar flares and cosmic energies due to a shielding effect caused by its close proximity to Earth.

11. Sun and planets, notably Jupiter, Saturn, Uranus, and Neptune, have a dominant effect on the energy particles reaching Earth.

There are other forms of energies in the universe still undiscovered reaching Earth and affecting human life.

Effect of Cosmic Energy on Human Life

Science has not been able to create living cells or organisms. Science, with all its advances, cannot bring back life into a dead body. Physics deals with explaining the features of nature and the universe with hypotheses and theories, but the life energy, consciousness, or soul remains unexplained. Molecular biology focuses exclusively on researching the building blocks of nature, losing sight of the characteristic differences between living and dead matter. For molecular biology, there is no qualitative difference between a living and a dead cell; a cell still contains the same molecules and structure. But what has happened in between the living and the dead cell? What caused the change? What is the living force? This needs a paradigm shift in the current approach of science, a new revolutionary thinking and approach. The intent of this chapter is to discuss some of these questions and present how biophysics, biophotons, and biofield may be the new science to answer these questions. One of the founders of quantum mechanics, Erwin Schrödinger, has said:

> *The soul is the greatest of all cosmic wonders; it is the "conditio sine qua non" of the world as an object. It is remarkable that Western mankind, with a few exceptions, has accorded so little value to this fact. The flood of external objects of cognizance has made the subject of all cognizance withdraw into background, and often into apparent nonexistence.*

Let us now discuss how cosmic energies reaching Earth impact human life. First we need to understand biophysics, biophoton, and biofield.

Biophysics

Biophysics (also biological physics) is an interdisciplinary science that applies the theories and methods of physics to questions of biology.[54] Biophysics removes the traditional barriers between physics, chemistry, biology, and medicine. Models and experimental techniques of physics (e.g., electromagnetism and quantum mechanics) are applied in biophysics to understand the function of living cells, tissues, and organs.

One area of research in biophysics is the absorption and emission of light by molecules. Light is an electromagnetic wave with a wide spectrum. Ultraviolet (UV) and visible light constitute only a small fraction of the electromagnetic spectra. The energy of a photon (E) depends on its frequency f, given by the formula $E = h.f$, where h is the Planck's constant. A photon of the gamma ray end of the spectrum has energy of about 10^{-13} joule, whereas a photon near the radio end of the spectrum has energy of only 10^{-28} joule. Thus, there is an enormous difference between the energies of photons from different parts of the electromagnetic spectrum. The energies involved in most chemical reactions are of the order of $2 \times 10^{-19} - 2 \times 10^{-18}$ joule per molecule. Photons in the UV and visible part of the spectrum have energies that are in this range. From this, it can be concluded that the photons in the visible range and lower range of UV are involved in photobiological and photochemical reactions. Chemical bonds are primarily interactions between electrons. Hence, the energy due to absorption of photons causes redistribution of electrons in the molecule.

Thus, photons in the visible region and lower range of UV have the ability to cause chemical reactions when they are absorbed. By contrast, photons in the x-ray and gamma ray have so much energy that they can blast a molecule apart into ions and electrons, and they are named ionizing radiation. Disciplines such as radiation physics, radiochemistry, and radiation biology are involved in the practice and research of interaction between ionizing radiation and matter.

Photons of the infrared and microwave radiation have little energy to cause any change in the molecule but induce changes in which the molecules vibrate and rotate. Detailed research investigations on infrared absorption have led to an extensive knowledge of the properties and structures of molecules. Thus, a particular effect of a photon on a molecule depends solely on its energy.

The ultraviolet (UV) region of the electromagnetic spectrum is especially harmful to living organisms. In human body, prolonged exposure to solar UV radiation may result in acute and chronic health effects on the skin, eye, and immune system. It can cause skin cancer. Fortunately for us living on Earth, the intense solar UV ray is mostly filtered by the ozone layer of the atmosphere and very little UV ray reaches Earth.

An important area in the study of molecular damage by UV is concerned with deoxyribonucleic acid (DNA), the genetic-carrier molecule. The human body has trillions of cells; each cell contains forty-six chromosomes, twenty-three from the mother and , twenty-three from the father. Chromosome contains about twenty-five thousand genes. Each gene is made of DNA which determines everything from eye color to IQ to many of the diseases we develop. Each DNA is composed of four types of molecules, called nucleotide base pairs: adenine, cytosine, guanine, and thymine. In these pairs, adenine always pairs with thymine; and cytosine always pairs with guanine.

It has been found that the wavelength of UV that was most efficient in causing cell death is precisely the wavelength that DNA absorbed most efficiently. These photoreactions in the DNA can create several photoproducts; the most damaging of them is the pyrimidine dimer. They are premutagenic lesions altering the structure of DNA. If they are not repaired, these lesions inhibit transcription and replication. Great deal of research work is going on currently to explore this area further.

Significance of Radiation

Radiation can be due to either the high energy particles or the high energy photons. As radiation passes through matter, events such as ionization of atoms and molecules cause a loss of energy, limiting the range of the radiation through the matter. In general, the more massive the energy of the radiation, the shorter the range. Thus, alpha particles have the shortest range, followed by beta particles and gamma rays, if initially they were equally energetic. As an example, the mean range in human tissue for 5.3 MeV alpha particles (quite energetic) is about 30 μm. This short range means that externally originated alpha particles rarely cause a health hazard. But gamma radiation accompanying the alpha decay may cause a health concern.

The mean range of 5.3 MeV electrons in human tissue is about 2.7

cm. The maximum path length will be about twice this figure (i.e., 5.4 cm). Most of the energies given up by the alpha or beta particles are used to create ion pairs at about 34 eV per ion pair. Thus the 5.3 MeV electron can create about 1.56×10^5 ion pairs along its total path length of 5.4 cm, or 3 ion pairs μm^{-1}. Many living cells are a few micrometers long, and several ion pairs can be created in the cell during the passage of an electron.

Damage to biological bodies occurs because molecules within the cells are altered as radiation passes through the cells. A bond in the DNA may be broken due to ionization by radiation. Some species have special mechanisms by which damage to one strand of DNA can be repaired, but the repair mechanism may not have time to operate if the cell is in rapid growth.

Biophoton

A biophoton[55] is a photon of light emitted from a biological system. This should not be confused with bioluminescence, which is the production and emission of high intensity light by deep sea marine lives. A biophoton emission is a very low intensity photon emission from living systems. Further terms used for this emission are ultra-weak bioluminescence, dark luminescence, and ultra-weak chemiluminescence. The typical magnitude of biophotons in the visible and ultraviolet spectrum ranges from a few up to several hundred photons per second per square centimeter of surface area. This is much weaker than the normal bioluminescence, but stronger than the thermal radiation that perfect black bodies radiate.

The first systematic research into the existence of light in the living systems was done by Russian scientist Alexander Gurwitsch. In the 1920s, Gurwitsch reported ultra-weak photon emissions from living tissues in the UV range of the spectrum. He named them "mitogenetic rays" because he assumed that they had a stimulating effect on cell division rates of nearby tissue. This approach to biology came under fierce attack by contemporary proponents of genetics and molecular biology. Consequently, the mitogenetic radiation hypothesis was largely ignored.

In the 1950s, a group of Italian astronomers developed a very sensitive photo multiplier that they used to make distant stars visible. When used on biological samples, it was shown that leaves, corn, beans, wheat germs, and so on emit a constant but weak light. This finding caused a brief uproar in the West but was soon forgotten.

In the 1970s, German physicist Fritz-Albert Popp and his research group at the University of Marburg, Germany, offered more detailed analysis. Popp and his colleagues built a highly sensitive light amplifier as shown in Figure 6.6. This can reliably measure

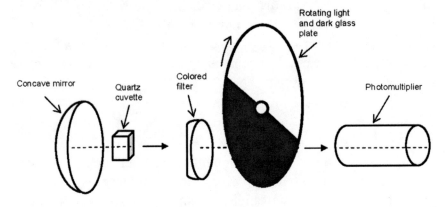

Figure 6.6: Schematic of Popp's light amplifier

the extremely weak light emission of biological samples. A quartz cuvette with probe is placed before a concave mirror in the enclosed apparatus, which directs the reflected rays to the light detector. A colored filter selects specific wavelengths, and the light and dark glass plate allows a separation between actual signals from the probe and spurious light from the apparatus itself.

Popp and his group showed beyond any doubt that low-level light emissions are a common property of all living cells. They showed that the spectral distribution of the emission falls over a range of wavelengths, 200 to 800 nano meter, which falls within the visible and UV range of the electromagnetic spectrum. Popp further proposed the hypothesis that the radiation might be both semiperiodic and coherent.

Implications of Biophotons

F.B. Ursini, R. Pelosi, and G. Benassi[56] have shown that the chemiexcitation process is a contributing factor to spontaneous biophoton emission. Chemiexcitation via oxidation stress by reactive oxygen species leads to the formation of triplet excited species, which release photons upon returning to a lower energy level. C. A. Boveris, E. Reiter, R. Filipkowski, M. Nakasi, and Y. Chance[57] have supported this further by studies indicating that emission can be increased by addition of reactive oxygen species.

Proponents of biophotons now suggest that biophoton emissions may be part of a system of cell-to-cell communication, which may be of greater complexity than the modes of cell communication currently known. Hence, biophotons may be important for the development of organs and tissues. Studies have shown that injured cells have a higher biophoton emission rate than normal cells. Hence, organisms with illness send a distress signal by emitting brighter light.

S. Cohen and F. A. Popp[58] investigated thoroughly biophoton emissions by the human body. Their investigation found that biophoton emission reflects:

1. left-right symmetry of the human body.

2. biological rhythm, such as fourteen days, one month, three months, and nine months.

3. disease in terms of broken symmetry between the left and right side.

4. light channels in the body, which regulate energy and information transfer between parts.

The results provide a new power tool of noninvasive medical diagnosis in terms of basic regulatory functions of the body.

Biofield

A biofield in the realm of spirituality and alternative medicine is claimed to be "a massless field" that (a) is not necessarily electromagnetic, (b) surrounds and permeates living bodies, and (c) affects the body. Although scientists and physicians remain skeptical about its existence, alternative medicine practitioners claim that a person has a field external from the body that strongly affects actions and feelings. They believe biofields can be degraded by EMF frequencies and electronic screens, such as radio waves, television, and computer screens and can lead to disease, overstress, and fatigue.

A well-known controversial approach for visualizing biofields of living organisms[59] was discovered by Semyon Kirlian in 1939. Kirlian found that if an object on a photographic plate is connected to a source of high voltage, small corona discharges (produced by the strong electric field at the edges of the object) creates an image on the photographic plate.

From the wave particle duality of quantum mechanics, emission of biophotons generates electromagnetic field, which may be the source of a biofield or human energy field.

On average, every human being consists of ten trillion cells. In every person, approximately ten million cells die every second and must be replaced in a short period of time in order to prevent an entropic decay. The replacement rate of the cells cannot be higher or lower than the decay rate; it must be exactly the same rate. Otherwise, the body would disintegrate quickly. If the growth rate in the intestinal cells exceeds the cell death rate, it will cause death due to obstruction of the intestines.

Hence, all these complex operations in a living body must occur in a very precisely controlled way. There must be an intimate cell-to-cell communication occurring at the speed of light, as pointed out by physicist Fritz Popp. Any other means of information transmission, including biomolecules, chemical messengers, and others would not be sufficient. They would be too slow to guarantee the integrity of operation. Biophotons, as described earlier, are now considered as the potential source of cell-to-cell communication.

Vital energy, or life force, or biofield energy has been discussed in great detail by various cultures in the past. This has been called by different names in different cultures: prana in Hinduism in India, chi or qi in China, ki in Japan, ankh in ancient Egypt, arunquiltha by the Australian aborigines, mana in Polynesia, pneuma in ancient Greece, tane in Hawaii, orenda by the Iroquois, and so on.

Hypothetical Cosmic Model of Natal Chart

There is vast amount of scientific research and concrete evidence supporting the influence and effects of cosmic energies on human life. Cosmic energies reaching Earth come from galaxies and stars. Known cosmic energies are the baryons (notably protons and electrons), and electromagnetic waves (gamma rays, x-rays, visual lights, infrared rays, etc.). But baryons comprise only 4% of the universe. We still do not know anything about the dark matter and dark energy, which comprise 22% and 74% of the universe, respectively.

Because biophotons are responsible for cell-to-cell communication, any disruption of biophotons by external energies will cause illness and disease. This is what alternative medicine calls as imbalance of energy. Hence, cosmic energies are bound to affect human life, positively or negatively.

In 1938, Maki Takata at Toho University in Japan began a biochemical study of the variation in rate for the precipitation of albumin in the blood. It turned out that the rate of the reaction varied with the time of day, the date of the year, the eleven-year sunspot cycle, eclipses, and magnetic storms in Earth's ionosphere. Up until this time, scientists believed it to be an ironclad law that if a series of identical chemical reactions was performed under the same set of conditions (heat, light, purity, humidity, etc.), each reaction would proceed at the same rate in any geographical location. Clearly, celestial influences were exerting a powerful influence upon the protein in the blood. Takata knew that proteins are the only chemical substances capable of "life," as we know it, on Earth, and here he had demonstrated in his test tubes that celestial influences were affecting the chemical behavior of this protein.

Proteins belong to a group of substances known to chemists as colloids. In 1951, at the University of Florence in Italy, Giorgio Piccardi became interested in Takata's work and decided to repeat the Takata experiments, this time using a nonbiological colloid called oxychloral bismuth, which is prepared by dissolving trichloral bismuth in water. Piccardi discovered that the speed of this oxychloral bismuth reaction also varied according to celestial conditions. Unusual sunspot activities, eclipses, and magnetic storms tended to interfere with and slow down the reaction, while periods of lesser cosmic activity tended to speed it up. In 1954, Caroli and Pichotka in Germany followed the work of Takata and Piccardi and demonstrated again that the rate of reaction varied with time and celestial conditions.

The cosmic energies reaching Earth have two sources: cosmic energies originating outside the solar system and cosmic energies originating from the solar flares of the Sun. The cosmic energies that reach Earth affect human biofields. When the cosmic rays and particles that originate outside the solar system enter the solar system, they are influenced by the Sun, Moon, and planets. These cosmic particles and rays reaching Earth are affected by (a) the magnetic field of the Sun, Moon, and planets, (2) radiation and solar wind of the Sun, (3) the charged ionosphere of the planets, (4) magnetospheres of the planets, (5) the dust devils of Mars, and (6) the shielding effect of the Moon and other nearby planets. Table 6.2 gives the attributes of the Sun, Moon, and planets, which will influence the cosmic energies that originate outside the solar system.

Table 6.2: Factors affecting cosmic energies in the solar system

Celestial Bodies	Distance from Earth Million Miles	Diameter miles	Gravity w.r.t. Earth's g	Magnetic field	Magneto-sphere	Emission
Sun	93	86,400	28g	Very strong and complex depends on sunspots and solar flares	Extending well beyond Pluto	Heat, light, and solar flares of of electrons, protons, x-ray, UV ray, gamma rays
Moon	0.239	2,158	0.16g	None	None	Reflected sun light
Mercury	57	3,000	0.38g	1% of Earth's		Deflects solar wind
Venus	26	7,700	0.91g	Weaker than Earth's	Weak	
Mars	49	4,219	0.38g	None	None	Occasional dust devil storms of charged particles
Jupiter	391	89,000	2.54g	19,500 times stronger than Earth's	Strong, deflects solar wind	
Saturn	793	75,100	1.08g	570 times stronger than Earth's	Deflects solar wind	
Uranus	1,691	31,585	0.91g	Tilted 59° from the axis of rotation, 40 times stronger than Earth's	Strong, deflects solar wind	
Neptune	2,700	31,000	1.19g	Tilted 47° from the axis of rotation, 27 times stronger Earth's	Resembles that of Uranus	
Pluto	3,573	1,470	0.08g	Not known	Not known	

As can be seen from the Table 6.2, the Sun has by far the biggest influence, followed by Jupiter, Saturn, Uranus, Venus, Mercury, and Mars. Pluto has virtually no effect on cosmic energies. Moon's effect is mainly due to its gravity and shielding, caused by its proximity to Earth.

So we have now two factors, as follows:

1. The cosmic particles and rays are controlled by the Sun, Moon, and planets.

2. The cosmic energies affect our biofield, which in turn affect our health and activities.

We can safely deduce now that the Sun, Moon, and planets are the contributing factors to the control of our health and activities.

In astrology also, the Sun, Moon, and planets affect human life and activities. But, astrology also includes Zodiacs, houses, and horoscope charts. Astrology also gives in detail the effect of planets and Zodiacs on characters and traits of a person. How do Zodiacs, the constellations on the ecliptic, affect us? How do we relate these details in astrology to the flow of the cosmic energies we know so far? The truth is that scientists know only 4% of the cosmic energies. Also, the research work on the biofield and biophoton is at a very early stage. Very little is known about the effect of cosmic energies on human life.

I will make some bold assumptions, as follows:

1. *Cosmic energies, known and unknown, have different types or flavors.*

2. *Each flavor of cosmic energy infuses certain specific qualities in a person.*

3. *Each Zodiac acts a filter and transmits a certain flavor of cosmic energy.*

Based on these bold assumptions, let us build a hypothetical cosmic model of the natal chart with the following suppositions:

1. Because each Zodiac acts as a filter and transmits a certain flavor of cosmic energy specific to the Zodiac, that flavor of energy affects the biofield of a person to infuse the attributes of the corresponding Sun sign in that person.

Astrological premise:

In astrology, a Sun sign represents the Zodiac in which the Sun resides at the time of a person's birth. The Sun sign attributes the qualities of a person. The Sun has the biggest influence on Earth and therefore, on humans, among all the celestial bodies.

Cosmic model assumption:

Cosmic energies have different flavors; each flavor incorporates different qualities in a person by affecting the person's biofield. Each Zodiac acts a filter for the cosmic energies that transmit only a particular flavor of cosmic energies.

2. The position of planets relative to the Sun at the person's birth time affects the cosmic energy flow; hence, it influences the character and well-being of the person.

Astrological premise:

The planets and the Moon influence the qualities of the Sun sign, depending on their position in the natal chart. If in conjunction with the Sun, they have positive influence. If in opposition to the Sun, they have negative influence.

Cosmic model assumption:

Jupiter and the Moon have the bigger influence, followed by Saturn, Uranus, Neptune, Mars, and Mercury.

3. The Moon and the planets affect the cosmic energy flow; hence, they influence the qualities of a person.

Astrological premise:

The planets and the Moon impart certain qualities in a person, depending on which Zodiac each is positioned.

Cosmic model assumption:

The planets and the Moon affect the flavor of cosmic energies transmitted by the Zodiac in which each is positioned.

A model based on these premises and assumptions is shown in Figure 6.7. In this model, the Sun is in Zodiac Virgo during birth. Hence, the Sun strongly influences the flavors of the cosmic energy transmitted by the Zodiac. Not knowing the nature of these cosmic energies, it is difficult to predict how they are traveling through the solar system to reach Earth. We have explained before that protons travel along the heliospheric current sheet, but whatever the travel path of the cosmic energies may be, as a landmark, the Zodiac that is in line with Earth and the Sun filters a certain flavor of cosmic energies,

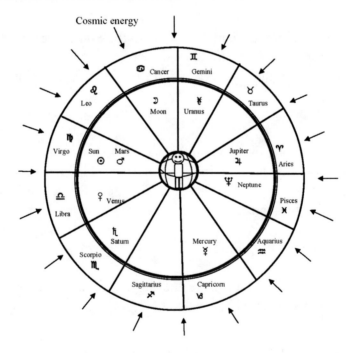

Figure 6.7: Hypothetical cosmological model of natal chart

which is enhanced by the Sun to infuse certain attributes associated with the Zodiac. Mars being in conjunction with the Sun enhances it further. The next powerful planet, Jupiter, is placed in Zodiac Aries. Here again, Jupiter influences the faculties associated with

Aries, which are caused by the related flavor of the cosmic energies. Similarly, we can explain the faculties associated with the other planets placed in the Zodiacs, although their influence will be less than the Sun's and Jupiter's.

Concluding Remarks

Cosmic energies reaching Earth (and therefore, humans) are controlled by the Sun, the Moon, and the planets in the solar system, depending on their position relative to Earth. Hence the Sun, Moon, and planets influence the body and mind of person. This is similar to the tenets in astrology.

It has been scientifically proven that human cells have biophotons generating a biofield. Cosmic energies influence the biofield with a positive or negative effect on the body and mind. This is similar to the ancient belief of prana or chi in the human body. Biophotons and the biofield are a new branch of science. As new results and discoveries appear in this area, we will be able to understand more and more about the effect of cosmic energies on the human body and mind.

Scientists know very little of the cosmic particles and energies of the universe. Baryons, which comprise only 4% of the total, are known. Nothing is known so far about the dark matter (22%) or dark energy (74%). Extensive work is going on in astronomy, cosmology, and atomic physics to explain dark matter and dark energy. A new collider, called the Large Hadron Collider (LHC) was built by the European Organization for Nuclear Research (*Organisation européenne pour la recherche nucléaire*), commonly known as CERN. It is the world's largest particle physics laboratory, situated in the northwest suburb of Geneva on the border between France and Switzerland. This may reveal new subatomic particles that may explain the mysteries of dark matter and dark energy. The astrological community should keep a close eye on the results of the experiments. Newly discovered particles and energies may provide further insight into the relationship between human behavior and cosmic energies.

As new results and discoveries appear, we will understand more and more about the effect of cosmic energies on the human body and mind.

The controls of life are structured as forms and nuclear arrangements, in a relation with the motions of the universe.

—Louis Pasteur

Chapter 7
The Basis of Astrology is Similar to Quantum Mechanics

I think it is safe to say that no one understands quantum mechanics.

—Richard Feynman

In this chapter I will discuss the fifth good reason why astrology is a science: the basis of astrology is similar to quantum mechanics. I will describe how quantum mechanics evolved to explain atomic and subatomic structures, the basics of quantum mechanics, and the similarity between quantum mechanics and astrology.

Classical Physics

Classical physics explains all physical phenomena with two entities: matter and energy. Drop a stone from a bridge; it falls because Earth's gravitational force pulls it. The stone is matter; force is energy. We strike a billiard ball with a cue. Knowing the position of the ball, the force applied, the direction of the force, and the mass of the ball, we can precisely calculate where the ball will be after certain time. Classical physics started from Isaac Newton, the greatest creative genius science had ever seen before Einstein. Newton's great masterpiece *Principia* has probably had a greater influence in our civilization than any other book except the Bible. Albert Einstein, the greatest scientist after Newton, wrote this appreciation of Newton:

> *In one person he combined the experimenter, the theorist, the mechanic, and not least, the artist in exposition.*

There is a popular story that Newton was sitting under an apple tree; an apple fell on his head, and he suddenly thought of the universal law of gravitation. As in all such legends, this is almost certainly not true in its details, but the story contains elements of what actually happened. Probably the more correct version of the story is that Newton, upon observing an apple fall from a tree, began to think along the following lines: the apple is accelerated, as its velocity changes from zero as it is hanging on the tree and moves toward the ground; thus, there must be a force that acts on the apple to cause this acceleration. He called this force *gravity*, In his later years, Newton was asked how he had arrived at his theory of universal gravitation. "By thinking on it continually" was his response. "Continual thinking" for Newton was almost beyond mortal capacity, with nonstop passion and obsession, living without food or sleep, on the edge of a breakdown.

Newton's three laws of motion provide relationships between the motion of a body and the forces acting on the body. The first law states that if a body is at rest, it will be resting unless acted upon by an external force. Thus, a stone in the garden will be there forever unless an external force, caused by an event, moves it. The second law states that if a body is acted upon by an external force, it will accelerate in the direction of that force. The acceleration will be proportional to the force and inversely proportional to the mass of that force. If a truck and a Toyota car each stalled on a level road, it will take many more people to push the truck—that is, to accelerate it from rest—than to get the Toyota car moving to the same velocity. This is because the truck has a greater mass than the Toyota, and the force required is directly proportional to the mass to have certain acceleration. The third law states that the reaction is equal in magnitude and opposite in direction. Thus, when I sit on a chair, I am pressing my weight on the chair. The chair is pushes back with equal force, and I sit comfortably. If I push harder than the chair can push back, the chair will collapse. If the chair were to push back harder than I push on it, then I would fly into the air. By the third law, equilibrium is reached, and no harm is done.

Newton postulated that light is composed of particles, or *corpuscles*, and investigated the refraction of light, demonstrating that a prism decomposes white light into a spectrum of colors, and that a lens and a second prism could recompose the multicolored spectrum into white light. He also showed that the colored light does not change its properties, regardless of whether it is reflected or scattered or transmitted. From this work, he concluded that any refracting telescope would suffer from the dispersion of light into colors, and he invented a reflecting telescope (today, known as a Newtonian telescope) to bypass that problem. Newton postulated the existence of ether as a media to transmit light.

Newton had difficulty explaining diffraction and interference of light with his corpuscular theory of light. Diffraction is the slight bending of light as it passes around the edge of an object. Interference is the pattern developed due to superposition of two waves. This was solved by English scientist Thomas Young, who postulated a wave theory of light by his famous double-slit experiment, demonstrating that light does travel in waves.

U.S. scientist Benjamin Franklin conducted extensive research in electricity, including his famous kite-flying experiment. It sparked the interest of later scientists, whose work provided the basis for modern electrical technology. Most notably, these include Italian physicist Luigi Galvani, Italian physicist Alessandro Volta, English physicist Michael Faraday, French physicist André-Marie Ampère, and German physicist Georg Simon Ohm.

Magnets were known from very early times. In the early nineteenth century, scientists discovered connections between electricity and magnetism. An electric current flowing through a wire produces magnetic field around it. The reverse is also true. The Scottish physicist James Clerk Maxwell showed mathematically that electric and magnetic fields travel through space in the form of waves and at the constant speed of light. The traveling electric and magnetic waves are called electromagnetic waves. Maxwell's contributions to physics are considered by many to be of the same magnitude as those of Isaac Newton and Albert Einstein.

Albert Einstein (1879–1955), born in Ulm, Germany, is the greatest physicist of all time. In popular culture, the name "Einstein" has become synonymous with genius. After graduation, unable to get a teaching job, Einstein took a job as a patent examiner at the Swiss patent office in Berne in 1902. During the seven years he spent at this office, Einstein laid the foundations of much of twentieth-century physics. In 1905 , while working at the patent office, Einstein published four revolutionary papers in *Annelen der Physik*, the leading German physics journal.

All four papers are today recognized as tremendous achievements—and hence, 1905 is known as Einstein's "Wonderful Year." At the time, however, they were not noticed by most physicists as being important, and many of those who did notice them rejected them outright. Einstein's first postulate states that all observers moving at constant speeds, even if those are different from each other, must witness the identical laws of physics. A body moving at a constant speed has no acceleration and is said to be in an inertial frame. All observers moving at constant speeds (i.e., in inertial frames) will obtain the same results involving the same masses, lengths, areas, magnets, and so forth. All speeds are relative; absolute speeds do not exist. Thus, when we are traveling in a train, we find that the train is moving relative to the houses or trees by the side of the rail track. If we just look at another person or picture inside the train, we would not see that the train is moving. This is the first principle of relativity.

Einstein's second postulate states that the speed of light is always measured as the same by all observers, independent of their own motion or the motion of the emitting body. Thus, the speed of light in a vacuum is a universal constant c of value 2.9979×10^8 meters per second. Light is an electromagnetic wave. Consider the two postulates below:

1. Observers in constant speeds (inertial frames), having no acceleration, witness identical laws of physics.

2. The speed of light is constant, independent of the motion of the observer or the body emitting the light.

For everyday life, the ordinary velocities of planes, cars, trains, bullets, and so on, the velocity is so much smaller than the speed of light that the time dilation is not noticeable. But as the velocity approaches the speed of light, the effect become enormous. Now, what is the effect of time dilation? Consider the following example: Sam and Bob are twins. Sam is an astronaut and goes on a space trip with a time clock. Bob and his time clock stays on Earth. When Sam returns to Earth, he is younger than Bob, and his time clock reads an earlier time than Bob's clock. This means that Sam has aged less than his twin brother, Bob. Now, if Sam travels in the space module at nearly the speed of light and returns from a distant planet after few months in his time measurement, he might find that his great-grandchildren have died of old age. A real paradox!

Einstein's theory of relativity also creates a contraction of length. Again, for everyday situation, the velocity is so much smaller than the speed of light that the length contraction is not noticeable and can be totally ignored. However, as the velocity approaches the speed of light, the length contraction is quite noticeable.

Another postulate of the theory of relativity is an increase of the mass of an object with speed. When the object is moving, the mass increases but very slightly, at ordinary speed. But as its speed approaches the speed of light, its mass increases significantly.

In another brilliant paper in 1905, Einstein proposed another revolutionary theory: the mass of a body is equivalent to a very concentrated form of energy, according to his famous equation: $E = mc^2$; where E is the energy, m is the mass of a body, and c is the velocity of light. Since c^2 has an immense magnitude, this mass-equivalent energy is also immense. To get an idea of this immense energy, to supply the energy need of a city with a population of three million, it would need mass-equivalent energy of a body of mass 33 grams. The energy of an atomic bomb explosion comes from converting some mass directly into energy.

We can now summarize the three results of Einstein's special theory of relativity.

1. Time inside a moving frame is slower than the time inside a frame at rest.
2. The length of a moving body gets shorter.
3. The mass of a moving body gets heavier.

A special theory of relativity deals with bodies moving at a constant velocity and does not deal with acceleration. Now, we know that gravity generates acceleration. Einstein suddenly thought about this relation between gravity and acceleration when he was sitting in a chair in the patent office: "If a person falls freely, he will not feel his own weight." This simple thought made a lasting impression on him, and he went on to publish the general theory of relativity in 1915, which became the most successful gravitational theory, being almost universally accepted and widely supported by observations.

In the general theory of relativity, gravity is not really a force; it is a manifestation of the curvature of space/time (note: not space but space/time—this distinction is crucial). Now what is space/time? If we toss a ball, it travels a short distance in space but an enormous distance in time, as one second equals about 300,000 kilometers in units where $c = 1$. Thus, a slight amount of space/time curvature has a noticeable effect.

The curvature of space/time can be viewed intuitively in the following way: If we place a heavy object, such as a bowling ball, on a trampoline, it will produce a dent in the trampoline. This is analogous to a large mass such as Earth causing the local space/time geometry to curve.

The larger the mass, the bigger the amount of curvature. A relatively light object placed in the vicinity of the dent, such as a ping-pong ball, will accelerate toward the bowling ball in a manner governed by the dent. Firing the ping-pong ball at a suitable combination of direction and speed toward the dent will result in the ping-pong ball's orbiting the bowling ball. This is analogous to the Moon orbiting Earth.

In the general theory of relativity, massive objects do not directly impart a force on other massive objects, as hypothesized in Newton's laws of gravity. Instead, in a manner analogous to the ping-pong ball's response to the bowling ball's dent rather than the bowling ball itself, other massive objects respond to how the first massive object curves space/time.

Problem with Classical Physics

A problem came with the classical physics in explaining the black-body radiation. In physics, a black body is an object that absorbs all electromagnetic radiation that falls onto it. No radiation passes through it, and none is reflected. It is this lack of both transmission and reflection to which the name refers. A black body represents a system in which the thermal energy is carried via electromagnetic radiation. Hence, it is possible to approximate the temperature of the object through the wavelength of the electromagnetic radiation that is emitted. Black bodies below around 430° C produce very little radiation at visible wavelengths and appear black (hence the name). Black bodies above this temperature, however, produce radiation at visible wavelengths, starting at red, going through orange, yellow, and white, before ending up at blue as the temperature increases.

In the laboratory, a black-body radiation is approximated by the radiation from a small hole entrance to a large cavity. Any light entering the hole would have to reflect off the walls of the cavity multiple times before it escaped, in which process it is nearly certain to be absorbed. This occurs regardless of the wavelength of the radiation entering (as long as it is small compared to the hole). The hole, then, is a close approximation of a theoretical black body and, if the cavity is heated, the spectrum of the hole's radiation (i.e., the amount of light emitted from the hole at each wavelength) will be continuous and will not depend on the material in the cavity.

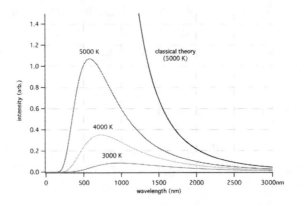

Figure 7.1: Black-body radiation curve at different temperatures

The black-body radiation at different temperatures is shown in Figure 7.1. As can be seen, each curve has a definite peak. It passes through a maximum intensity at a certain frequency and then declines, but according to Raleigh-Jeans law in classical physics, the intensity keeps on increasing with frequency, as shown in Figure 7.1 for radiation at 5000 K. This has been called ultraviolet catastrophe.

It remained for the German physicist Max Planck (1858–1947) to solve the problem. Planck introduced an equation for the radiation with a constant called Planck's constant, *h*. In classical physics, it was always assumed that the difference in energy radiated by two atoms could be as small as we chose. Planck's law provides a lower limit to that difference. Thus, continuous gradation of energy is replaced by the discrete stepwise change of energy. Thus, the energy emitted by the light particle photon is $E = h\nu$, where E is energy, h is Planck's constant, and ν is frequency. The Planck constant has dimensions of energy multiplied by time and is expressed in joule seconds (J·s). The value of the Planck's constant is:

$$h = 6.62606896 \times 10^{-34} \ \text{J.s}$$

Planck calculated that the number of photons is fewer as the energy level is higher. Hence, there are fewer photons at the ultraviolet frequency, solving the ultraviolet catastrophe.

Photoelectric Effect

Planck's constant helped solve the puzzle of photoelectric effect. When weak red light shines on a cesium surface, a few slow electrons are emitted. If the red light is made brighter, more electrons are emitted, but they still travel slowly. If a dim blue light is used, there are few electrons emitted, but they travel faster. If the blue light is made brighter, more electrons are emitted, but their velocities remain the same. If infrared light is used, no electrons are emitted. These phenomena cannot be explained by the wave theory of light developed by Maxwell and Fresnel.

Einstein solved this puzzle by assuming that the incident light was quantized, and light was made of particles called photons. He used the equation $E = h\nu$, where E is the energy of photon, h is the Planck's constant, and ν is the frequency of the incident light. Cesium atoms that are hit by photons emit electrons. Blue photons have more energy (hence, more velocity) than the red photons, as the blue light has higher frequency than the red light. From the viewpoint of classical physics, emitted electron velocity ought to increase with increasing incident light intensity, regardless of the light's frequency.

What happens now with the wave theory of light? We will see the duality of wave and particle when we discuss quantum mechanics.

Bohr's Atomic Structure

If an electron is orbiting around the nucleus, then the electrical force of attraction between the negatively charged electron and the positively charged proton in the nucleus will force the electron to collapse into the nucleus. Danish physicist Niels Bohr (1885–1962) overcame this difficulty by introducing discrete energy levels of the electrons by using Planck's constant. Bohr has been called the "Great Dane," "the spirit of modern physics," "the founder of quantum mechanics," and so on, in recognition of his outstanding contributions, which were dwarfed only by Einstein.

The spiraling of the electron into the nucleus is due to the continuous change in its motion, as permitted by classical laws of physics. But if the electron can change its state of motion in discrete steps, it must then stay in a particular orbit until it emits or absorbs enough energy in one single process to go from one orbit to another. This, then, leads to discrete orbits, and transitions from one orbit to another give results in either the absorption or emission of discrete energy levels.

Bohr's atomic theory successfully explained the atomic structure of hydrogen, but when it came to atoms of other elements, his theory was not sufficient. This is when quantum mechanics came into the picture.

Quantum Mechanics

Quantum mechanics is the science of matter and radiation at atomic and subatomic levels. Classical physics failed to explain small particles. The term *quantum* (Latin for quantity) refers to the discrete quantities that the theory assigns to physical items, such as the energy of light and electromagnetic wave. Quantum mechanics includes the following attributes:

1. Laws of probability

2. Discreteness of energy

3. Wave-particle duality

4. Schrödinger equation

5. Uncertainty principle

6. Exclusion principle

7. Spin of a particle

I will now discuss each item in detail.

Laws of Probability

Probability is the likelihood that a certain thing will happen. The probability theory is used extensively in statistics, mathematics, science, and philosophy to draw conclusions about the likelihood of potential events and the mechanics of complex systems.

Consider this example: According to the theory of probability, the probability that a coin, when tossed, will come up heads is exactly one-half, or 50%. Now, if we flip a coin ten times, we may get heads only three times. Again, if we repeat flipping the coin ten times, this time we may get heads six times. So where does this probability of 50% come from? It means that the result of any toss is uncertain. But if we flip the coin enough times—say, a million times—we will find that heads shows up very close to 50% of the time.

Another example: When tossing a pair of dice, what is the probability of throwing a seven in the next dice throw? There are six sides to each of the two die. If we assume equal chances for each side, we get 6 x 6—or 36—equally probable outcome configurations. Six of these configurations will add up to seven as follows:

one for die #1 and six for die #2
two for die #1 and five for die #2
three for die #1 and four for die #2
four for die #1 and three for die #2
five for die #1 and two for die #2
six die #1 and one for die #2

So the probability of getting a seven in the next dice throw is six out of thirty-six, or 16.6 percent. Gamblers may make money by taking advantage of odds, calculated by this method.

The fundamental principle of quantum mechanics is based on the law of probability, not the law of certainty. Let us look at the picture of an atom in its ground state. If we think that the electron is looping around the nucleus, as shown in Figure 7.2, then we are eighty years out of date. According to quantum mechanics, the probability density plot of the electron in an atom is shown in Figure 7.3. The density of the dots represents the probability of finding the electron in that region.

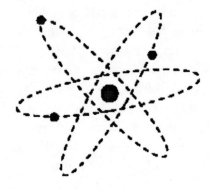

Figure 7.2: Electron looping around the nucleus according to classical physics.

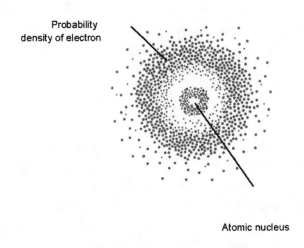

Figure 7.3: Electron probability density cloud according to quantum mechanics.

The size of an atom is ~1 x 10^{-10} meter. The central nucleus, where 99.9 percent of the atom's mass resides, is ~1 x 10^{-15} to 1 x 10^{-14} meter. The size of an electron is not exactly known, but the classical electron radius is thought to be of the order of 2.8 x 10^{-15} meter. If the nucleus were the size of our Sun, then the hydrogen ground state would be twenty times larger than the solar system. If the electron were really a point particle moving around the atomic space, it would reside in a space so vacant that it would make the solar system seem crowded. Now, if we consider the wave function of the electron with its probability density, then the probability density will fill up the whole atomic space. For instance, try to push your hand through a wall. Because atoms are mostly empty space, their electrons are too small to stop you. But the probability density clouds of the atoms push your hand back. Pretty effective, aren't they?

Discreteness of Energy

This has been discussed in the section on Bohr's atomic structure, where we saw that electrons can exist only at discrete energy levels.

Wave-Particle Duality

While physicists were puzzling over the light's seemingly contradictory properties, waves and particles, French physicist Louis de Broglie (1892–1987) hypothesized that all entities have both wave and particle aspects. De Broglie pointed out that a photon's wavelength, a wave property, could be related to the photon's momentum, a particle property, by combining $E = h\nu$ with another energy equation:

$$E = mc^2$$

As we have discussed earlier, E is the energy, h is the Planck's constant, ν is the frequency, m is the mass, and c is the speed of light. Combining the two equations, we get:

$$E = h\nu = mc^2$$

From which, we obtain:

$$mc = \frac{h\nu}{c}$$

Because the photon's speed is *c*, the term *mc* in the equation above can be regarded as the photon's momentum *p*, hence:

$$p = \frac{h\nu}{c}$$

Now, we know that $\lambda\nu = c$, which connects the wavelength λ, frequency ν, and speed of light *c*. Hence:

$$\nu = \frac{c}{\lambda}$$

Substituting the value of ν, $p = \dfrac{h\nu}{c} = \dfrac{h}{\lambda}$

This equation proves that the momentum (which relates to a particle) is inversely proportional to the wavelength (which relates to a wave), thus showing the wave-particle duality. This equation refers to photons, but de Broglie saw no reason why electrons and other particles of matter should not also have associated frequencies and wavelengths.

Confirmation of the wave nature of electron, as hypothesized by de Broglie, came in 1928 from the experiment demonstrated by two American physicists, Clinton Davisson and Lester Germer. In their experiment, an electron beam of a precisely determined low energy was formed and directed at a prepared face of nickel crystal, and scattered portions of the beam were collected by a movable detector. They found that electrons were not scattered uniformly in all directions. Instead, under certain conditions, a sharply defined current of electrons was observed in a direction for which the angle of incidence on the crystal's surface was equal to the angle of reflection. If the nickel surface were entirely smooth and flat to the electrons, this result would have been expected. But to particles like electrons, the nickel surface cannot conceivably be smooth, as the size of an electron is much smaller than the size of the atom of nickel. To solve the mystery, Davisson and Germer assumed that the electrons have wavelike structures and applied Bragg's law of diffraction for scattering of x-rays from a crystal lattice. British physicist Lawrence Bragg treated x-rays as waves and derived a famous equation in the analysis of an x-ray diffraction pattern. The application of the same equation by Davisson and Germer in explaining the diffraction pattern of electrons confirmed the wave nature of electrons.

Schrödinger's Equation

Austrian physicist Erwin Schrödinger (1887–1961) invented a differential equation to derive wave functions for electrons. When the equation is solved, it yields a set of wave function represented by Greek letter Ψ (psi). According to the equation, electrons confined in their orbits would set up standing waves and would describe the probability where an electron could be. For a single electron in a free atom, the wave function square Ψ^2 measures the probability of finding the electron at or near a given location. The larger the value of Ψ^2, the greater the probability of finding the electron at that location. The distribution of these probabilities forming regions of space around the nucleus are called orbitals. Thus, orbitals could be called an electron density cloud. The densest area of the cloud has the greatest probability of finding an electron, and the least dense area has the lowest probability of finding an electron, as shown in Figure 7.13.

Uncertainty Principle

German physicist Werner Heisenberg (1901–1976) proposed the uncertainty principle for the quantum mechanics, stating that the position and momentum of a particle cannot be accurately determined simultaneously. If the position of the particle is accurately known, then the speed and direction of the speed will have poor accuracy. This is because the measurement itself changes the position, speed, or direction of the particle. This is not obvious in the macroscopic world around us. If we want to measure the length of a table with a tape, the measurement does not change the length or position of the table in our acceptable measuring capacity. In the case of electron, measurement becomes different. The very act of looking at the electron with a super-high-power magnifier uses light made of photons. These photons would have enough momentum that they once hit, the electron would change its course. Heisenberg wrote the uncertainty principle as:

$$\Delta p \Delta x = \hbar \quad \text{.................................. Equation 3.21}$$

On the right side is the Planck's constant divided by 2π (called reduced Planck's constant).Momentum is represented by p, and position (distance) is represented by x. The Δ symbols mean uncertainty of, not change of. Hence, Δx is the uncertainty of position, and Δp is the uncertainty of momentum. Since $\hbar$ on the human scale is extremely small, Δx and Δp are, for all practical purposes, zero in the everyday world.

Exclusion Principle

The Pauli exclusion principle is a quantum mechanical principle formulated by Austrian physicist Wolfgang Pauli (1900–1958) in 1925. This principle is significant, because it explains why matter occupies space exclusively for itself and does not allow other material objects to pass through it, while at the same time allowing light and radiation to pass. It states that no two identical fermions—electrons, protons, and neutrons are fermions—may occupy the same quantum state simultaneously. For electrons in a single atom, it states that no two electrons can have the same four quantum numbers. The Pauli exclusion principle is one of the most important principles in physics, primarily because the three types of particles from which ordinary matter is made—electrons, protons, and neutrons—are all subject to it; consequently, all material particles exhibit space-occupying behavior.

The Pauli exclusion principle helps explain a wide variety of physical phenomena. One such phenomenon is the rigidity or stiffness of ordinary matter (fermions). The principle states that identical fermions cannot be squeezed into each other—material objects collide rather than passing straight through each other, and we are able to stand on the ground without sinking through it. Another consequence of the principle is the elaborate electron shell structure of atoms and of the way atoms share electron(s) and a variety of chemical elements and their combinations (chemistry). An electrically neutral atom contains bound electrons equal in number to the protons in the nucleus. Because electrons are fermions, the Pauli exclusion principle forbids them from occupying the same quantum state, so electrons have to pile on top of each other within an atom.

Spin of a Particle

Atomic particles possess an intrinsic angular momentum or spin. The spin is quantized. The spin is just a convenient way of describing the angular momentum of a particle. In magnetic resonance imaging (MRI), the spin of the hydrogen atom is flipped to detect the presence of water. Because tumors have a different concentration of water from the surrounding tissue, they would stand out in such a picture.

Quantum numbers

The Bohr model was an one-dimensional model that used one quantum number to describe the distribution of electrons in the atom. The only information that was important was the size of the orbit, which was described by the n quantum number. Schrödinger's model allowed the electron to occupy three-dimensional space. It therefore required three coordinates, or three quantum numbers, to describe the orbitals in which electrons can be found. The three coordinates that come from Schrödinger's wave equations are the principal (n), angular (l), and magnetic (m) quantum numbers. These quantum numbers describe the size, shape, and orientation in space of the orbitals on an atom.

To distinguish between the two electrons in an orbital, we need a fourth quantum number. This is called the spin quantum number (s) because electrons behave as if they were spinning in either a clockwise or counterclockwise fashion. One of the electrons in an orbital is arbitrarily assigned an s quantum number of +1/2; the other is assigned an s quantum number of -1/2. Thus, it takes three quantum numbers to define an orbital but four quantum numbers to identify one of the electrons that can occupy the orbital.

Debate on Quantum Mechanics

The extraordinary success of quantum mechanics in applications did not overwhelm everyone. A number of scientists, including Schrödinger, de Broglie, and—most prominently—Einstein, remained unhappy with the standard probabilistic interpretation of quantum mechanics. Einstein to Bohr: "God does not play dice with the universe." Bohr to Einstein: "Stop telling God how to behave." While their actual exchange was not quite so dramatic and quick as the paraphrase would have it, this was nevertheless a wonderful rejoinder from what must have been a severely exasperated Bohr.

The Bohr-Einstein debate had the benefit of forcing the creators of quantum mechanics to sharpen their reasoning and face the consequences of their theory in its most starkly nonintuitive situations. The foundations of the subject contain unresolved problems; in particular, problems concerning the nature of measurement. An essential feature of quantum mechanics is that it is generally impossible, even in principle, to measure a system without disturbing it. The detailed nature of this disturbance and the exact point at which it occurs are obscure and controversial. In spite of the indeterminacy, the physicists who explain the mysteries of atomic and subatomic particles are still pursuing quantum mechanics unhesitatingly.

Einstein and his two junior assistants, Boris Podolsky and Nathan Rosen, proposed a thought experiment (known as EPR experiment) to contradict the tenet of quantum mechanics. The EPR experiment is proposed in the following manner: Consider a pair of electrons, A and B. According to quantum mechanics, the two electrons are identical except that they have opposite spins—spin up and spin down. Hence, the sum of the angular momentums of the two electrons is zero. If we measure the momentum of electron A, we instantly know the momentum of electron B, as their sum is zero even without measuring it. But B can be light-years away, and no signal can travel faster than light, according to Einstein's theory of relativity. This shows that the two, quantum mechanics and Einstein's paradigm, are not compatible. This was further confirmed by Irish mathematician John Bell by his theory of inequalities. So, which is right—quantum mechanics or Einstein's paradigm?

In 1982, A. Aspect, P. Grainger, and G. Roger, working at the University of Paris, created pairs of photons and sent members of each pair to detectors separated by a distance of thirteen meters. The detectors measured the polarization of the photons, a property related to their spin. This team showed that measuring the polarization of photons at one detector affected the polarization measured at the other detector. The influence that traveled between the detectors did so in less than ten nanoseconds. This was a quarter of the time less than a light signal would have taken to travel the thirteen-meter distance. If the team had the technology to measure an even smaller time interval, they could have found that this unknown influence traveled even faster. Hence, quantum mechanics is right, and, alas, Einstein's paradigm is wrong.

But is there is a signal that travels faster than light? In the experiment done by Aspect, et al., the two photons were not separate in the first place. They had the same potential. In the world of potentiality, they were not two photons but just one potentiality with manifestation for both. In the potential world, they are united as one. Hence, they are interconnected beyond the limits of space and time. This is known as the theory of entanglement, which states that even though particles appear separated on the subatomic level, they, in fact, resonate together. That even if a particle is placed on one side of the universe and another is placed at the opposite side, they would resonate instantaneously when one is caused to vibrate.

Similarity between Astrology and Quantum Mechanics

Like quantum mechanics, astrology is also based on probability.[60] Astrologers collected data thousands of years ago on how certain patterns of Zodiacs and planets provided certain attributes. A Sun sign represents the Zodiac in which the Sun resides at the time of a person's birth. For example, the attributes of a person with Sun sign Aries are leadership, energy, aggressiveness, courage, confidence, arrogance, and belligerence. It does not mean that every Aries person will have these attributes. It means that the probability of an Aries person having these attributes is higher than for other Sun signs. The actual figure of probability is not quoted so far but only can be calculated statistically from very large numbers of collected data.

The uncertainty principle of quantum mechanics applies to astrology as well.[60] The Sun sign of a person means that in the Zodiac of the Sun sign, the Sun and Earth are in line. The energy particles from and through the Sun sign Zodiac and from the Sun reach Earth and affect the people born at that time. But the energy particles on their way to Earth can be impacted by the electromagnetic fields and gravitational fields in the path, as well as the solar system. Thus, there is some uncertainty in how many of these energy particles can reach Earth. Similarly, there are some uncertainties on the attributes assigned to the Sun signs. These attributes are based on the collected data so far. How extensive the data collection has been is not known, and the attributes may change as more data are collected. If the uncertainty of the energy flow is ΔE, and the uncertainty of the assigned attributes are ΔA, then:

$$\Delta E \ \Delta A \ = \text{astrology error}$$

Heisenberg wrote the uncertainty principle as:

$$\Delta p \Delta x = \hbar$$

On the right side is the reduced Planck's constant (i.e., Planck's constant divided by 2π). Momentum is represented by p, and position (distance) is represented by x. The Δ symbols mean uncertainty of, not change of. Hence, Δx is the uncertainty of position, and Δp is the uncertainty of momentum. As we see from Heisenberg's equation, the multiplication of the uncertainties of position and momentum in quantum mechanics equals Planck's constant divided by 2π. In the case of astrology, the values of astrology error and its constancy are not known. But what is accepted so far is that there is a margin of error in astrology analysis and prediction.

Wave-particle duality equally applies for the cosmic energies, because the same particles and energies are in astronomy as are in cosmology.

The attributes of an electron are contextual,[60] depending on how they are measured. An example of a contextual attribute is the color of an object. If you go to a shop to buy a dress, the color of the dress you choose will depend on the light in the shop. If the dress you choose is white but the light in the shop is bluish, then the dress will have a bluish tinge. Moreover, if you are wearing tinted glasses, then the color of the dress will also depend on the tint of your glasses. Hence, the contextual attributes of an object depend on the environment and the person observing or measuring it. The contextual attributes in quantum mechanics apply to astrology as well. If the astrology prediction is that a person is going to win some money, then for a poor person living in poor neighborhood, winning one hundred dollars may be substantial, and the neighbors might congratulate him. But for a rich person living in rich neighborhood, this amount may be insignificant and will go unnoticed by the neighbors. Hence, the effectiveness of the prediction depends on the environment and the observers.

No one has yet claimed to understand quantum mechanics, but it has been successful so far in explaining the behavior of particles at the atomic and subatomic level. Niels Bohr said: "Anyone who is not shocked by quantum theory has not understood a single word." Einstein never accepted the probability theory of quantum mechanics. He had constant debates with Niels Bohr about quantum mechanics, but they agreed that somehow quantum mechanics explains the behavior of atomic and subatomic particles.

Couldn't the same thing be said about astrology? The first thing that should be realized is that astrology is not certainty but probability. The second thing is that the astrology is based on the data collected over a certain period a few thousand years ago. That data collection has not continued; hence, astrology attributes have not been updated. Astrology has not been accepted as science by the scientific community. In order to get astrology accepted as science, its basis should be similar to quantum mechanics: (1) duality of cosmic energies as particles and waves, (2) probability, not certainty, (3) uncertainty principle of cosmic energy flow and human attributes, and (4) contextual attributes.

Even though the theory of entanglement may not directly apply to astrology, it does support the idea that although there is no visible connection between us and the celestial bodies, the possibility exists that two independent bodies (planets and humans) can resonate together in unison, due to entanglement.

Concluding Remarks

Quantum mechanics has been successful so far in explaining the behavior of atomic and subatomic particles, which classical mechanics could not. But no one fully understands quantum mechanics. Schrödinger said, "Had I known that we were not going to get rid of this damned quantum jumping, I never would have involved myself in this business." This shows the frustration of one of the founders of quantum mechanics with the inexplicability of quantum mechanics. Eminent American physicist John Wheeler said, "If you are not completely confused by quantum mechanics, then you do not understand it."

According to quantum mechanics, it is not possible to exactly locate an electron. We can only know the probability of an electron being at a certain place. If we want to know precisely the speed of an electron, we would not know the precise location of the electron, and vice versa. Quantum mechanics does not provide certainty but only probability. There is no exact one-to-one relationship between cause and effect; there is always some uncertainty.

In astrology there also is no certainty but only probability. Astrology does not provide, with certainty, that the positions of the planets and celestial bodies cause specific malefic and benefic effects on human life; it offers probability that the effects might happen. Due to a current lack of detailed scientific knowledge of cosmic energy and its effect on human life, astrological prediction becomes more uncertain. Similar to quantum mechanics, there is no one-to-one cause-and-effect relationship in astrology; there is always some uncertainty.

Astrology and quantum mechanics have a similar scientific basis.

> *To our classical sensibilities, the phenomena of quantum mechanics—interference, entanglement, nonlocal correlations, and so forth—seem weird. The various formulations package that weirdness in various ways, but none of them can eliminate it because the weirdness comes from the facts, not the formalism.*

> —Daniel Styer, et al. *American Journal of Physics.*

Chapter 8
Conclusion

The cosmos is a vast living body, of which we are still parts. The sun is a great heart whose tremors run through our smallest veins. The moon is a great nerve center from which we quiver forever. Who knows the power that Saturn has over us, or Venus? But it is a vital power, rippling exquisitely through us all the time.

—D.H. Lawrence

Astronomy, cosmology, and physics study the celestial bodies and energies in the universe and their interaction among them. Astrology studies the effect of celestial bodies and energies on humans and earthly affairs. Hence, there should be no conflict between these branches of science. Both the scientific community and the astrological community must understand this and avoid the ongoing mud-slinging.

Hypothesis or theory cannot be proven; it can only be invalidated. Any independent scientific researcher who is not pressured by financial sponsors will accept that it is impossible to prove absolutely that a theory is correct; one can prove only that it is possible that it is not invalid. Astrology has not been scientifically shown to be invalid. Certain phenomena cannot be explained scientifically, but that does

140

not mean that a phenomenon does not exist. Force of gravitation existed before Newton created the law of gravity, and Einstein further modified it with the general theory of relativity. There are many phenomena in the universe still undiscovered and unexplained. Science cannot insist these phenomena are phony.

Science can be classified into following three categories:

1. Natural science: an empirical study dealing with a body of facts or truths systematically arranged and showing the operation of general rules or laws

2. Mathematical science: a priori study that is predominantly concerned with abstract formal systems; for instance, logic, mathematics, theoretical branches of computer science, information theory, and statistics

3. Social science: study of human behavior and society

Because astrology assumes and attempts to interpret the influence of celestial bodies on human affairs, the definition of social science is applicable to astrology.

In a behavioral science such as economics or astrology, we also deal with causes and effects in a broader sense—not one to one—and we make hypotheses to state which causes can produce which effects. Economist Amartya Sen proposed the concept of capability as a social indicator in the development of economics. Capability depends on functioning, which includes literacy and positive freedom (a person's ability to do something) in developing countries. But it is not possible to state in precise terms how much economic growth is achieved by literacy. This is because we are dealing with a very large population—the entire population of a country. Also, it is difficult to isolate other causes for economic growth in a country that may include foreign investment, a sudden drop in the prices of oil and gas, world economy, etc. The parallel with astrology is now obvious:

• Astrologers are dealing with the entire human race and all its activities.

- The existing state of knowledge in the physical sciences cannot yet identify or isolate the forces in nature by which heavenly bodies influence human activities.

Economics is science because it deals with statistical correlation and derives specific conclusions. That astrology pursuing the same path has yet to be recognized as science.

What is the success rate of a long-term weather forecast—monthly, yearly, or even weekly? The weather forecast for the next few days has a better success rate, but that rapidly decreases for weekly, monthly, and yearly forecasts. This is in spite of meteorological research that uses advanced computers and satellites. This does not mean that meteorology is not science. It means that the troposphere condition, which determines the weather pattern, is dependent on the solar system. Hence, there are lots of variables to take into account when making the weather forecast—a very difficult task. In the case of astrology, the task is even more daunting, as the variables include the solar system as well as the celestial bodies outside the solar system. Curiously, the scientific community is noticeably silent about the results of meteorology but is very critical of astrology.

Medical science made enormous progress in the twentieth century. New drugs, antibiotics, and vaccines are now available to cure many diseases that have been responsible for epidemics and numerous deaths. Surgeons perform complex operations, such as heart transplants and brain surgery, which were never thought possible in an earlier era. Current medical treatments are becoming more specialized, focusing on only a certain organ or part of a body. When treating a certain disease, the doctors mostly examine the organ or the part of the body related to the disease. This is different from the treatment by the doctors of alternative medicine, who consider the state of the whole body and mind of the patient in diagnosing the disease.

Astrology is based on statistical analysis. Astrology is social science. Astrology is linked with alternative medicine. Astrology is explained by cosmic energy and the biofield. And the basis of astrology is similar to quantum mechanics, These five good reasons given in the previous chapters to justify astrology as a science—social science—should convince the readers and the scientific community. As Carl Jung stated in a letter to L. Oswald on December 8, 1928:

> *Astrology is knocking at the gates of our universities. A Tubinger professor has switched over to astrology, and a course on astrology was given at Cardiff University last year. Astrology is not merely superstition but contains some psychological facts (like theosophy) which are of considerable importance.*

Astrology is based on data collected thousands of years ago on celestial bodies and their relationship to humans and earthly affairs. Since then, no new data have been collected. Hence, the astrology practice has remained unchanged. This is due to (1) lack of financial support to carry out research, (2) lack of collective mutual support of astrologers to share their knowledge and experience, and (3) not considering astrology as a social science.

For money to be available to fund research in accredited institutions, a donor or corporation or industry has to make a contribution. Do most benefactors, directly or indirectly, control and dictate what the funds are used for? Yes! In today's world, it is unlikely that an individual or a corporate donor will designate funds toward astrology research; this is not the area that will be acclaimed by the scientific community or support the marketing of corporate promotional efforts.

Most practicing astrologers today are driven to earn money without considering the value of astrology as science. They hesitate to share their knowledge with others, fearing that it may jeopardize their practice and earnings. They do not keep track of their clients and find out how their assessment and prediction compare with the actual outcome. This lack of feedback keeps their method and technique unchanged. So whatever they have learned in the beginning, from whatever source it might be, does not improve or modify. This is a dangerous practice and is the major reason why astrology has remained unchanged for thousands of years.

Astrologers must be especially careful in predicting the future. Predictive astrology is the most complex area of astrology. It needs detailed analysis of the natal chart, transits, and progressions, which cannot be done in few minutes, as is done by most of the practicing astrologers. Genuine and quality astrology does not concern itself exclusively with prediction. Many consultants use natal charts exclusively for character analysis and counseling and refuse to have anything to do with forecasting. They advocate that character itself will shape the future, and that when a strong individual will is involved, hard-and-fast predictions are meaningless.

Astrology is only one of the factors determining the character and traits of a person. Others factors are inherited genes, family, society, and environment. That is why identical twins can develop different characters if they are separated and brought up in different societies and environment.

Why is the popularity of astrology and alternative medicine increasing, in spite of the rapid advance of science and technology? There are two reasons: (1) people see the benefit to their health and mind, and (2) current science and technology are purely materialistic; they do not address the vital life energy or spiritual side. Astrology and alternative medicine effectively function in these areas with proven success. Most people, whether they admit it or not, read the star column in the daily newspaper before starting the day or heading for work. Most magazines have astrology sections with weekly or monthly forecast. In India, natal charts and astrology predictions are used widely for match-making of brides and grooms.

Astrologers have to take advantage of this recent upsurge of interest in astrology for the enhancement and improvement of astrology, with extensive research work as follows:

1. Data from the study of the natal charts of the clients should be collected and followed by statistical analysis of the collected data to find a pattern. This idea was started by Michel Gauquelin with considerable success. There should be a central databank where all practicing astrologers and consultants could enter the astrology data of their clients. The data should include the following: (a) Sun signs and the characters of the clients, (b) methods of astrology prediction, and (c) astrology predictions for the clients and the actual outcomes after follow-ups with the clients.

2. The attributes of the Sun signs and planets should be regularly updated after detailed statistical analyses of the data stored in the databank. This should be carried out by an expert panel assigned by the astrology community.

3. The astrology community should work closely with alternative medicine practitioners for mutual benefit. Both astrology and alternative medicine are based on the concept of life energy. Alternative medicine practitioners sometimes consult the natal chart for the diagnosis of the patient's ailment. The information from these practitioners would be valuable data for the statistical analysis of astrology.

4. Psychologists and social scientists would obtain valuable information on the character and behavior of their clients by studying the natal charts of the clients. Astrologers could get feedback from psychologists and social scientists on how the astrology information of the clients matches with the actual behavior and character of the clients. In this way, astrology should be included in social science. Four current communities—astrologers, alternative medicine practitioners, psychologists, and social scientists—should work together to obtain grants from donors and corporate sponsors to carry out research work on the subject of astrology's benefiting alternative medicine, psychology, and social science.

5. Biofield and biophotons are new areas of science that have just started to be explored. Research work in these areas in universities and research institutions should be encouraged, with very exciting prospects and results benefiting every branch of science, including astrology, alternative medicine, and psychology. The astrology community should keep abreast of all new findings in these areas, and see how these findings can further explain the relationship between cosmic energies and human behavior.

6. Extensive work is being conducted in astronomy, cosmology, and atomic physics to explain dark matter

and dark energy. The Large Hadron Collider (LHC) in the European Organization CERN (*Organisation europeene pour la recherche nucleire*) for Nuclear Research may reveal new subatomic particles that help to explain the mysteries of dark matter and dark energy. The astrology community should keep a close eye on the results of the experiments. Newly discovered particles and energies may provide further insight into the relationship between human behavior and cosmic energies.

I have explained five good reasons why astrology—the oldest known science—deserves a place in social science. Astrology is not competing with natural science. Although astrology and astrology had the same root, they branched out, with astrology focusing on the relation between celestial bodies and individuals. Astrology study provides probability not certainty, based on statistical analysis. As astronomy and cosmology explore the universe to find out more about its origin and composition, we should also know how the celestial bodies and cosmic energies affect individuals. By using statistical techniques and newfound knowledge of cosmic energies, the biofield, and biophotons, astrology will help us understand much more about the relationship between celestial bodies and individuals.

The question of all questions for humanity, the problem which lies behind all others and is more interesting than any of them, is that of the determination of man's place in nature and his relation to the cosmos.

—T.H. Huxley

Men should take their knowledge from the Sun, the Moon, and the stars.

—Ralph Waldo Emerson

Astrology is a fact, in most instances. But astrological aspects are but signs, symbols. No influence is of greater

*value or of greater help than the will of an individual. ...
Do not attempt to be guided by, but use the astrological
influences as the means to meet or to overcome the faults
and failures, or to minimize the faults and to magnify the
virtues in self.*

—Edgar Cayce

Appendix 1:   Planet Attributes in Zodiacs

Planet	Zodiac	Attributes
Sun	Aries	Action, leadership, energy, aggressive, courage, will power, confidence, arrogant, combative, impulsive
	Taurus	Stable, reliable, steady, practical, material possessions and money, slow to start, but steady progress, loyal, stubborn
	Gemini	Most intelligent, quick mind, curious, multi-tasking, versatile, wit, restless, communication, can be shallow, lacks self-discipline
	Cancer	Most sensitive, intuitive, domestic matters very important, caring, tenacious, endurance, moody, clinging to loved ones
	Leo	Noble, generous, leadership, confident, ambitious, attraction to opposite sex, ego, outspoken, ostentatious, domineering
	Virgo	Perfectionist, efficient, thorough, analytical, adaptable, pettiness, critical and seeking flaws of others
	Libra	Partnership, joint enterprise, harmonious, balance, fairness, hardworking, diplomat, indecisive, overly romantic
	Scorpio	Strong will power, workaholic, resourceful, intense dedication, vindictive, jealous, intense emotion, never gives up, strong sex drive
	Sagittarius	Good fortune, abundance, optimistic, friendly, sociable, honest, charming, idealistic, generous, giving advice, blunt, tactless
	Capricorn	Frugal, hardworking, responsible, desire for status, patient, persistent, reserved, secretive, condescending, lacking integrity
	Aquarius	Freedom, independence, unconventional, humanitarian, inventiveness, originality, stubborn, eccentric, dogmatic
	Pisces	Intuitive, sensitive, sympathetic, romantic, compassionate, strong imagination, charitable, easily influenced, not ambitious, stubborn
Moon	Aries	Aggressive, confident, energetic, action oriented, decisive, combative, blunt
	Taurus	Cautious, trustworthy, hardworking, stable, stubborn, mother's influence
	Gemini	Articulate, dashing, restless, witty, versatile, curious, mother's influence
	Cancer	Affectionate, sentimental, moody, maternal, nurturing, loves children
	Leo	Confident, happy, pride, ambitious, creative, easily hurt
	Virgo	Industrious, practical, helpful, well ordered, shy, fussy
	Libra	Gracious, kind, romantic, diplomatic, even tempered, balanced
	Scorpio	Passionate, controlling, willful, intense emotion, easily hurt, jealous
	Sagittarius	Philosophical, cheerful, generous, optimistic, outspoken, mother's influence
	Capricorn	Ambitious, reserved, materialistic, hard working, mother's influence
	Aquarius	Unconventional, wants freedom, difficulty in showing emotion
	Pisces	Musical, artistic, or poetic ability; compassionate, very sensitive, easily hurt

Planet	Zodiac	Attributes
Mercury	Aries	Lightning-fast mind, impatient, competitive, irritable, dominant, exciting
	Taurus	Conservative, sensible, inflexible, good manager, shrewd in business
	Gemini	Quick thinker, inventive, perceptive, intellectual, communicator, actor
	Cancer	Sensitive, intuitive, home important, communicative, amazing memory
	Leo	Leadership, ambitious, creative, confident, boastful, communicative
	Virgo	Smart, persistent, knowledgeable, analytical, thinker, idealist, nitpicker
	Libra	Rational, balanced, prudent, hard working, slow in making decisions
	Scorpio	Resourceful, shrewd, analytical, intuitive, determined, detective, biting wit
	Sagittarius	Intellectual, communicative, humorous, wide-ranging mind
	Capricorn	Methodical, realistic, organized, rigid, pessimistic, communicative
	Aquarius	Thinker, brilliant, progressive, perceptive, humane, intuitive
	Pisces	Instinctive, amazing memory, receptive, empathetic, imaginative, illogical
Venus	Aries	Enthusiastic, excitable, impulsive, self-centered, affectionate, easily aroused
	Taurus	Affectionate, charming, artistic, sensual, security, musical
	Gemini	Conversant, flirtation, wit, indecisive mind, avoid lasting relationship
	Cancer	Kind, loyal, devoted to home and family, clinging to love and friend
	Leo	Warm, outgoing, family loving, creative, passionate, flamboyant, romantic
	Virgo	Critical, modest, controlling, do everything for lover, shy
	Libra	Affectionate, gentle, warm, attractive to others, aesthetic sense
	Scorpio	Proud, passionate, seductive, stormy love life, jealous, vengeful
	Sagittarius	Ardent, excitable, demonstrative, love freedom, sees love as adventure
	Capricorn	Ambitious, serious, sophisticated, controlling, value stability, hides emotion
	Aquarius	Open-minded, friendly, idealistic, independent, promiscuous
	Pisces	Sentimental, romantic, artist, devoted, composed, sacrifice for lovers
Mars	Aries	Energy, sexual charisma, assertive, leadership, courage, explosive temper
	Taurus	Hardworking, determined, persistent, down to earth, materialistic
	Gemini	High spirited, lively, ingenious, versatile, communicative, argumentative
	Cancer	Emotional, sensitive, possessive, protective, responsive
	Leo	Confidant, energetic, impassioned, leadership, will power, creative, arrogant
	Virgo	Hardworking, methodical, calculating, perfectionist, critical
	Libra	Friendly, charming, stylish, flirtatious, appealing, at a loss without partner
	Scorpio	Assertive, energy, emotion, will power, highly sexed, jealous, revengeful
	Sagittarius	Independent, enthusiastic, adventurous, strong conviction, determined
	Capricorn	Efficient, leader, ambitious, rise to the top, materialistic, cool temper
	Aquarius	Enterprising, unconventional, progressive, thinker, impatient
	Pisces	Generous, self-sacrifice, restless, intuitive, emotional, artistic, musical

Planet	Zodiac	Attributes
Jupiter	Aries	Confidence, energy, outgoing, education, spiritual matter
	Taurus	Devoted, kind, materialistic, sound judgment, commerce, business
	Gemini	Clever, multitalented, curious, writer, actor, leader
	Cancer	Benevolent, intuitive, sympathetic, business
	Leo	Magnanimous, compassionate, well liked, leadership
	Virgo	Organized, practical, perfectionist, intellect, internal tension
	Libra	Likable, fair, sympathetic, charming, difficulty in making decision
	Scorpio	Passionate, will power, aggressive, ambitious, reserved, sexual intensity
	Sagittarius	Genial, optimistic, generous, philosophical, tolerant, far-sighted
	Capricorn	Ambitious, dutiful, hardworking, serious-minded, pessimistic
	Aquarius	Open-minded, innovative, original, tolerance, egocentric
	Pisces	Sympathetic, forgiving, intuitive, self-sacrifice, creative, spiritual pursuit
Saturn	Aries	Independent thinker, determined, disciplined, forceful, assertive
	Taurus	Finance ability, frugal, practical, methodical, stubborn, prudent
	Gemini	Clever, articulate, problem solver, multiple interests, lucid mind, science
	Cancer	Difficult childhood, insecure, clingy in love, protective, nurturing
	Leo	Determined, dignified, need for recognition, arrogant, entertainment field
	Virgo	Analytical, industrious, worried, precise, gloomy
	Libra	Rational, reliable, diplomatic, fair, wealth, honor, late marriage
	Scorpio	Resourceful, hard driver, determined, ambitious, jealous, resentful
	Sagittarius	Honest, forthright, education, independence, firm beliefs, aspiration.
	Capricorn	Capable, ambitious, pragmatic, competent, disciplined, leader, hardworking.
	Aquarius	Original mind, liberal, organizer, principled, unselfish, scientific pursuit.
	Pisces	Sympathetic, intuitive, creative, neurotic, anxiety, afraid of isolation
Uranus	Aries	Independent, feisty, impatient, ingenious, flickering enthusiasm
	Taurus	Committed, will power, arts, music, financial ups/downs
	Gemini	Clever, inquisitive, nervous, versatile, talkative, communication
	Cancer	Sensitive, fluctuating mood in change, imaginative
	Leo	Ardent, talented, stubborn, demanding, enthusiastic
	Virgo	Analytical, practical, dynamic, restless
	Libra	Imaginative, artistic, relationship problem
	Scorpio	Emotional, strong willed, charismatic, resourceful, temper
	Sagittarius	Optimistic, independent, lively, travel, education
	Capricorn	Ambitious, responsible, individuality, thinker
	Aquarius	Tolerant, unsentimental, inventive, nonconformist, strikes of luck
	Pisces	Strange dreams, psychic, poor will power, art and religious pursuits
Neptune	Aries	Intuitive, spiritual creativity
	Taurus	Healing ability, preoccupation with finance
	Gemini	Clever, literary talent, may be shallow and unrealistic
	Cancer	Observant, receptive, sentimental, intuitive
	Leo	Extravagant, artistic, romantic, willing to take chances
	Virgo	Imaginative, anxious about details, hypochondriac

Planet	Zodiac	Attributes
	Libra	Idealistic, compassionate, lacking self-confidence
	Scorpio	Drawn to mystery, loose morals
	Sagittarius	Freedom, travel, enthusiastic
	Capricorn	Likes old-fashioned values and religion, creative
	Aquarius	Intuitive, strives for common good and social reform
	Pisces	Psychic, generous, mystical, gullible, passive
Pluto	Aries	Not known
	Taurus	Not known
	Gemini	Not known
	Cancer	Security paramount, intuitive
	Leo	Business skill, leadership
	Virgo	Obsessed with details, critical of others
	Libra	Obsessed with balance, beauty, and social relationship, arts
	Scorpio	Passionate, sexual, strong will power, resolute
	Sagittarius	Freedom, sensible, wise
	Capricorn	Not known
	Aquarius	Not known
	Pisces	Not known

Appendix 2:   Planet Attributes in Houses

Planet	House	Attributes	Strength
Sun	1	Leadership, strong will, energy, ambition, work hard, egoistic, pride, dominating	High
	2	Practical, persistent, financial interest and stability important	Medium
	3	Achievement by mental accomplishments, travel, siblings play important role	Medium
	4	Home and family central, early life struggle, prosperity in late life, intuitive	High
	5	Arts, literature and music careers, competitive, love children, happy, optimistic	High
	6	Distinction through work and service to others, delicate health	Medium
	7	Marriage and relationship important, sales person	High
	8	Emotional, interest in death and life after death, inheritance, finance	Medium
	9	Expand awareness through education, religion, philosophy and travel	Medium
	10	Ambition, work hard to achieve position and power, leadership	High
	11	High ideals, aspirations, friends, humanitarian	Medium
	12	Self-contemplation, work in science, medicine or institutions, spiritual activity	High
Moon	1	Desire for recognition, influenced by other people, impressionable, moody	High
	2	Business ability, need for financial security	Medium
	3	Strong imagination, skilled communicator, attachment to brothers and sisters	Medium
	4	Family relationship important, mother strong influence, need for security	High
	5	Romantic, talented, connects with children easily	Medium
	6	Need for productive and fulfilling job, unstable health	Medium
	7	Emotional fulfillment through marriage, need for job variety	High
	8	Intense emotion, sexual urge, psychic sensitivity	Medium
	9	Religious guru, philosopher, many travels	Medium
	10	Need for accomplishment and prominence, career essential	High
	11	Socially popular, friendship, politics	Medium
	12	Moody, sensitive, withdrawing, psychic ability	Medium
Mercury	1	Logical, very intelligent, communication, scholar, writer, scientist	High
	2	Business ability, original ideas, preoccupation with money	Medium
	3	Superior intelligence, problem solver, public speaker, writer	High
	4	Work out from home, interest in sciences, often leads nomadic life	High

Planet	House	Attributes	Strength
	5	Forceful and dramatic speaker and writer, loving bond with children	Medium
	6	Methodical, efficient, apprehensive; science, medical and sports career	High
	7	Good communicator, mediator, need caring relationship	High
	8	Intuitive, research skill in mysteries of life and death, secretive	Medium
	9	Interest in law, religion, higher education and philosophy, lots of ideas	Medium
	10	Good organizer, planner, leadership ability, public speaker, actor	High
	11	Group communication, work in literature, science and occult, eccentric	Medium
	12	Intuitive, psychic ability, secretive	Medium
Venus	1	Charming, friendly, romantic, impulsive, physical beauty for women	High
	2	Love of wealth, charming, seek wealthy partners, need security	High
	3	Good communicator, flirtation, love of literature, travel	Medium
	4	Love of home and family, devoted, clinging to loved ones	Medium
	5	Romance, optimistic, talents in arts, love of children	Medium
	6	Love of work, good relationship with boss and employees	Medium
	7	Good relationship with others, good marriage, business partnership	High
	8	Intense emotion, jealousy, seductive, financial gain through marriage	Medium
	9	Love of acting and philosophy, travel for pleasure, education, publishing	Medium
	10	Social ambition, arts profession, good relation with employers and opposite sex	High
	11	Many warm friendships, natural leader in group, open-minded, affectionate	Medium
	12	Compassion, love affair, love of solitude	Medium
Mars	1	Confidence, courage, leadership, aggressive, achieve high goals, combative	High
	2	Competitive, practical, financial gain, business	Medium
	3	Alert, quick-thinking, assertive, argumentative, impatient	Medium
	4	Dominating, protect home and family, strong physique	High
	5	Pursue love, sex, pleasure, and games, good athletes, love children	Medium
	6	Skilled people, surgeons, mechanics, engineers, danger of injury at work	Medium
	7	Aggressive, accomplishment, sales person, public relations, partnership	High
	8	Emotion, sexual desire, psychic, violent death, criminal tendency	Medium
	9	Crusader, social reform, independent thinker, intolerant of other beliefs	Medium
	10	Power position, executive ability, ambitious, become famous, leader	High

Planet	House	Attributes	Strength
	11	Aggressive, leader, revolutionary, demanding	Medium
	12	Secretive, losing identity, work behind scenes	Medium
Jupiter	1	Honest, truthful, popular, confidant, dignified, always protected	High
	2	Money and prosperity, business ability, desire to spend money	Medium
	3	Need for mental challenge, writing, publishing, travel, good relatives	Medium
	4	Harmony in family life, good fortune in later life, inheritance	High
	5	Teacher, counselor, love children, education, sports, arts	Medium
	6	Contribution to society, well liked, need to have the right job	Medium
	7	Good fortune through marriage and business partnership, kind, friendly	High
	8	Gain through inheritance, joint finance, investment and insurance	Medium
	9	High education, clergy, understanding, publishing, education, travel	High
	10	Success, fame in later part of life, ambitious, honest, high position, leadership	High
	11	Group activities, generous, help others, charitable	Medium
	12	Psychic, generous, introspective, prayer, need rejuvenation	Medium
Saturn	1	Cold, humorless, serious, reserved, hardworking, afraid of being hurt	High
	2	Hard work for living, frugal, shrewd in business	Medium
	3	Career in science, methodical, disciplined, communication, sibling rivalry	Medium
	4	Lack home security, isolation from parents	High
	5	Serious, career in entertainment and arts, responsible as parent	Medium
	6	Efficient, skilled, hardworking, worry about health	Medium
	7	Responsible, marriage with older mature partner	High
	8	Psychic, success in finance, problem with marriage	Medium
	9	High standard, teaching, publishing, law, religion, travel	Medium
	10	Success, recognition, politician, business executive, lack of integrity	High
	11	Work in groups and organization, traditional, ambitious	Medium
	12	Rarely recognized for work, stay in background	Medium
Uranus	1	Hate routine work, need constant change, adventure, eccentric, unconventional	Low
	2	Finance unsettling, money through invention in scientific field	Low
	3	Intuitive, innovative, brilliant mind, writer, thinker	Low
	4	Occult, change of residence, odds with parents	Low
	5	Unstable love life, wild creative streak	Low

Planet	House	Attributes	Strength
	6	Work in science, nerves affecting health	Low
	7	Unpredictable behavior, divorce in marriage	Low
	8	Occult, psychic ability, outrageous sex life, violent death	Low
	9	Unorthodox views, interest in occult and astrology, guru	Low
	10	Ultra liberal, radical, leader, entrepreneur, seek independence in job	Low
	11	Humanitarian, many friends	Medium
	12	Psychic, meditation, prefer solitude	Low
Neptune	1	Intuitive, hypnotist, artist, composer, must avoid drugs	Low
	2	Ability to earn money, extravagant, chaotic finance situation	Low
	3	Intuitive, occult, poetic ability, gullible	Low
	4	Emotional tie with family, psychic ability	Low
	5	Intuitive, music, art, stock market, secret relationship	Low
	6	Interest in medicine and music, spiritual healing, hypochondriac	Low
	7	Intuitive, psychic link, artistic, musical talent	Low
	8	Psychic, need care in business partnership	Low
	9	Interest in cult and mystic, need care against delusion	Low
	10	Intuitive, astrologer, clergy, psychiatrist	Low
	11	Generous, spiritual rapport	Low
	12	Intuitive, psychic, healing ability	Medium
Pluto	1	Individualistic, magnetic personality, strong will power, difficult to get along	Low
	2	Drive and ambition to get money, resourceful, may be selfish	Low
	3	Scientific ability, opinionated, position as spies, undercover agent, diplomats	Low
	4	Dominating family life, interest occult, geology and mining	Low
	5	Creative, sexual excess, gambling	Low
	6	Great focus and drive, work in atomic energy, need purpose in life	Low
	7	Attract powerful partner, dominating, position as judge and lawyer	Low
	8	Strong will, psychic, occult, intuitive, deeply serious	Medium
	9	Spiritual leadership, education, travel, tendency to become fanatic	Low
	10	Political leader, drive to succeed	Low
	11	Well respected, strong friendship	Low
	12	Intuitive, occult, act behind the scenes, private person	Low

Bibliography

1. Leo, Alan. *Casting the Horoscope.* Kessinger Publishing (2003).

2. Hewitt, William W. *Astrology for Beginners.* Llewellyn Worldwide (1992).

3. Oken, Alan. *Alan Oken's Complete Astrology.* Bantam Books (1980)

4. Das, Tapan. "Quantum Mechanics and Astrology." *Research in Astrology in Media in Science (RAMS),* Issue 13 (Sept 2005).

5. Blommers, Paul J., Robert A. Forsyth. *Elementary Statistical Methods in Psychology and Education.* University Press of America (1977).

6. "Michel Gauquelin," *Wikipedia, the free encyclopedia*

7. Gauquelin, Michel. *The Scientific Basis of Astrology.* Stein and Day Publishers (1969).

8. Eysenck, Hans, and David Nias. *Astrology: Science or Superstition* (1982).

9. Ertel, Suitbert. "Raising the Hurdle for the Athletes, Mars Effect: Association Co-Varies with Eminence." *JSE*, 2,1 (1988).

10. Ertel, Suitbert. *Society for Scientific Exploration.* Austin, Texas, Annual Symposium (May 1987).

11. Ertel, S. "Het weerbarstige Marseffect." *Skepter*, 45, (1996); reprinted in, "Debunking with caution - Cleaning up Mars-Effect Research." *Correlation,* 18, 9–41 (2000).

12. Ertel, S., and Ken Irving. *The Tenacious Mars Effect.* Urania, 36 (1996).

13. Muller, A., and S. Ertel. "1083 Members of the French Académy de Médecine." *Astroforschungsdaten,* vol 5.

14. Gauquelin, M. *Cosmic Influences on Human Behaviour.* Aurora Press (1994).

15. Torrey, E.F., J. Miller, R. Rawlings, and R. H. Yolken. "Seasonality of births in schizophrenia and bipolar disorder: a review of literature." *Schizophrenia Research*, 28(1), 1–38 (1997).

16. Chotai J., T. Forsgren, L. Nilsson, and R. Adolfsson. "Season of Birth Variations in the Temperament and Character Inventory of Personality in a General Population." *Neuropsychobiology*, 44, 19–26 (2001).

17. Yuan, Kathy, Lu Zheng, and Qiaoqiao Zhu. "Are Investors Moonstruck? Lunar Phases and Stock Returns." *The Journal of Empirical Finance*, 13(1):1–23 (2006).

18. Johnston, Brian T. "Planetary Aspects and Terrestrial Earthquakes." *ISAR International Astrologer* (2001).

19. Hill, Judith, and Jacalyn Thompson. "The Mars–Redhead Link: A Scientific Test of Astrology." *NCGR Journal. Winter* (1988–1989).

20. Ridgley, Sara K. "Astrologically Predictable Patterns in Work-Related Injuries." *Kosmos*, XXII[3], 21-30 (1993).

21. McRitchie Ken. "The Student's Critical Thinking Guide Regarding Science and Astrology." *ISAR International Astrologer*, 16:1.

22. McRitchie Ken. "Astrology and the Social Sciences. Looking in side the black of astrology theory." *Correlation: Journal of Research in Astrology*, Vol 24(1) (2006).

23. Jung, Carl G. *Synchronicity: An Acausal Connecting Principle.* Princeton University Press, (1973).

24. Perry Glenn. "The Essential Concepts in Psychological Astrology." *ISAR International Astrologer*, Volume 36, Issue 2.

25. www.solsticepoint.com/astrologersmemorial/eyesenck.html

26. Law, S.P. "The Regulation of Menstrual Cycle and Its Relationship to the Moon." *Acta Obstetricia et Gynecologica of Scandinavica,* 65, 45–48 (1986).

27. Criss, T.B., and J.P. Marcum. "A Lunar effect on Fertility." *Social Biology* 28, 75–80 (1981).

28. De Castro, J.M., and S.M. Pearcey. "Lunar Rhythms of the Mean and Alcohol Intake of Humans." *Physiology and Behavior,* 57, 439–444 (1995).

29. Neal, R.D., and M. Colledge. "The effect of the Full Moon on General Practice Consultation Rates." *Family Practice* 17(6), 472-474 (2000).

30. Lieber, A. "Human Aggression and Lunar Synodic Cycle." *Journal of Clinical Psychiatry,* 39(5), 385 (1978).

31. Tasso, J., and E. Miller. "Effects of Full Moon on Human Behavior." *Journal of Psychology* 93, 81-83 (1976).

32. Weiskott, G.N. "Moon Phases and Telephone Counseling Calls." *Psychological Reports,* 35, 752–754 (1974).

33. Hicks-Caskey, W.E., and D.R. Potter. "Weekends and Holidays and Acting-Out Behavior of Developmentally Delayed Women: A Reply to Dr. Mark Flynn." *Perception and Motor Skills*, 74, 1375–1380 (1991).

34. Campbell, D.E., and J.L. Beets. "Lunacy and The Moon." *Psychological Bulletin,* 85, 1123–1129 (1978).

35. Cyr, J.J., and R.A. Kaplan. "The Lunar Relationship : A Poorly Evaluated Hypothesis." *Psychological Reports,* 62, 683–710 (1987).

36. Rotton, J., and I.W. Kelly. "A Scale for Assessing Belief in Lunar Effects: Reliability and Concurrent Validity." *Psychological Reports,* 57, 239–235 (1985).

37. Vance, D.E. "Belief in Lunar Effects on Human Behavior." *Psychological Reports,* 76, 32–34 (1995).

38. Danzl, D.F. "Lunacy," *Journal of Emergency Medicine*, 5, 91–95 (1987).

39. Kelley, D.M. "Mania and the Moon." *Psychoanalytic Review* 9, 406–426 (1942).

40. Katzeff, K. "Moon Madness." *Citadel Press,* Secausus, N.J. (1981).

41. Szpir, M. "Lunar Phases and Climatic Puzzles." *American Scientist,* 86, 119–120 (1996).

42. Raison, C.L., H.M. Klein, and M.S. Teckler. "The Moon and the Madness Reconsidered." *Journal of Affective Disorders,* 53, 99–106 (1999).

43. Das, Tapan. "Letter to the Editor." *ISAR International Astrologer*, 36:1 (2008).

44. Marti, James. *The Alternative Health & Medicine Encyclopedia.* Visible Ink Press.

45. Rattenbury, Jeanne. *Understanding Alternative Medicine.* Franklin Watts (1999).

46. "Acupuncture." *Wikipedia, the free encyclopedia.*

47. Frantzis, Bruce. *The Big Book of Tai Chi.* Thomsons HarperCollins (2003).

48. "Big Bang," *Wikipedia, the free encyclopedia.*

49. Liddle, Andrew. *An Introduction to Modern Cosmology.* John Wiley & Sons (2003).

50. Das, Tapan. "Dark Energy and Primordial Energy." *Journal of the Mindshift Institute.*

51. "Electrical Dust Devils on Mars." http://www.thderbolts.info/tpod/2005/arch05/050321electridevils.htm

52. "Heliospheric Current Sheet." *Wikipedia, the free encyclopedia.*

53. Das, Tapan. "Energy Flow in Solar System Affecting Earth." *ISAR International Astrologer,* 35: 4 (2007).

54. "Biophysics." *Wikipedia. The free encyclopedia.*

55. "Biophoton." *Wikipedia, the free encyclopedia.*

56. Ursini F., R. Pelosi, and G. Benassi. "Oxidation Stress in the Rat Heart. Studies on Low Level Chemiluminiscence." *Journal of Bioluminiscence and Chemiluminiscence,* 4(1) (1989).

57. Boveris A. Cedenas, E. Reiter, R. Filipkowski, Nakase, and Y. Chance. "Organ Chemilumuniscence, Noninvasive assay for oxidative radical reactions." *Proceedings of the National Academy of Sciences,* USA, 77(1).

58. Cohen S., F.A. Popp. "Biophoton Emission of Human Body." *Indian Journal of Experimental Biology,* 41: 5 (May 2003).

59. Das, Tapan. "Cosmic energy controlled by planets and zodiacs affecting human life." *ISAR International Astrologer,* Volume XXXVI, Number 3 (2006).

60. Das, Tapan. "Similarity between Quantum Mechanics and Astrology." *Research in Astrology with Media in Science (RAMS)*, Issue 15 (July 2007).

Glossary

ACUPUNCTURE. An ancient Chinese technique of inserting needles in tiny points of the body for treating illness.

ALTERNATIVE MEDICINE. Any healing practice that does not fall within the realm of conventional medicine is termed as alternative medicine. Commonly cited examples include naturopathy, chiropractic, herbalism, traditional Chinese medicine, ayurveda, yoga, homeopathy, acupuncture, and tai chi.

ANGULAR HOUSE. In astrology, angular houses are first, fourth, seventh, and tenth houses.

ASCENDANT. In astrology, ascendant or rising sign is the Zodiac sign that is on the horizon (rising) at the person's moment of birth.

ASPECT PATTERN. Aspect is the relationship between two planets expressed in degrees and minutes at the birth moment of a person. Aspect pattern is a particular configuration of aspects combining three or more planets.

ASTEROID BELT. The region between Mars and Jupiter in the solar system is called asteroid belt. This region is composed of rocky bodies and asteroids.

AUTUMNAL EQUINOX. The ecliptic and celestial equator cross each other at two points called equinoxes. The equinox during September is called autumnal equinox.

AYURVEDA. It is the oldest known alternative medicine originated in India.

BARYON. Proton, neutron, and their antiparticles are baryons. In cosmology, electron, although fermion, is considered as baryon.

BIG BANG. Current accepted theory of the origin of universe is big bang, where an indescribable explosion occurred 13.7 billion years ago at trillions of degrees in temperature

BIOFIELD. A massless field, not necessarily electromagnetic, surrounding and permeating living bodies.

BIOPHOTON. A photon of light emitted from a biological system.

BIOPHYSICS. An interdisciplinary science that applies the theories and methods of physics to biological system.

BLACK BODY RADIATION. A black body absorbs all radiation and no radiation is reflected by it. In the laboratory, a black body radiation is approximated by the radiation from a small hole entrance to a large cavity.

CADENT HOUSE. In astrology, cadent houses are third, sixth, ninth, and twelfth houses.

CELESTIAL MERIDIAN. An imaginary great circle in the celestial sphere passing from the South point of the horizon, through the zenith to the north point of the horizon, and through the nadir.

CHI. In traditional Chinese culture, chi is the energy flow in a living body.

COSMIC ENERGY. Cosmic particles and rays from nova or supernova explosions and solar activities reaching Earth.

DARK ENERGY. Additional form of energy accounting for 70% of the mass of the universe.

DARK MATTER. Nonbaryonic matter in the galaxy.

DOSHA. Ayurvedic mind and body type.

ECLIPTIC. The path that the Sun forms during a year, as viewed from Earth.

EPHEMERIS. A table of values that shows where every planet was, is, and will be for every day past, present, and future.

FENG SHUI. An ancient Chinese practice of arranging objects (such as furniture) to help one improve life by receiving positive chi.

GRAND CROSS. An aspect pattern made up of four planets in a four cornered square that form four squares (90^0 apart) and two oppositions (180^0 apart).

GRAND TRINE. An aspect pattern when three planets form a triangle with trine (120^0 apart) aspects to each other.

HELIOSPHERIC CURRNET SHEET. A ballerina-skirt-like structure in the interplanetary magnetic field created by the oppositely directed open magnetic-field lines along the plane of the Sun's magnetic equator.

HOUSE. In astrology, the horoscope chart is divided into twelve equal houses with each house occupying 30 degrees of the circle.

HUBBLE CONSTANT. The radial velocity with which a galaxy recedes is linearly proportional to its distance. The proportionality constant is called Hubble constant.

INTERPLANETARY MAGNETIC FIELD. It is the part of the solar magnetic field that is carried into the interplanetary space by the solar wind.

KUIPER BELT. The region in the solar system beyond Pluto composed of icy objects.

KUNDALI. Indian horoscope chart.

MARS EFFECT. Michel Gauquelin found from his analysis that there were a significantly higher number of eminent athletes who had Mars in their horoscope charts either around the ascendant or the midheaven.

MERIDIAN (geography). An imaginary arc on the Earth's surface from the North Pole to the South Pole that connects all locations running along it with a given longitude.

MERIDIAN (Chinese philosophy). Energy channel in the body through which chi flows.

MERIDIAN (statistics). It is a point in a distribution of scores such that number of scores below it is the same as the number of scores above it.

MIDHEAVEN. Intersection of the celestial meridian with the ecliptic at birth.

MILKY WAY. The galaxy of our solar system.

NADI. The energy channel through which prana flows according to Indian philosophy.

NOVA. Nuclear explosion caused by the accretion of hydrogen onto the surface of a white dwarf.

PLANCK'S CONSTANT. Proportionality constant between the energy of a photon and the frequency of its associated electromagnetic wave.

PRANA. Life energy in Indian philosophy.

QUANTUM NUMBER. It describes the state of electrons in an atom according to quantum mechanics.

RED GIANT. It is a luminous giant star of low or intermediate mass that is in a later phase of its evolution.

SIDEREAL TIME. It is the time measured by the rotation of the Earth, with respect to the stars (rather than relative to the Sun).

SOLAR FLARE. It is a sudden local explosion in region of Sun's atmosphere caused by powerful local magnetic field.

SOLAR WIND. It is caused by a solar flare and contains a million tons of electrically charged subatomic particles leaving the Sun every second.

STELLIUM. In astrology, a group of three or more planets in conjunction in the same house is called stellium.

SUCCEDENT HOUSE. In astrology, second, fifth, eighth, and eleventh houses are succedent houses.

SUN SIGN. In astrology, Sun sign represents the Zodiac that the Sun is in at the time of a person's birth.

SUPERNOVA. A giant nova created by the collapse of a massive star or a white dwarf accumulating sufficient materials from a companion star.

TABLE OF HOUSES. It contains 360 charts with the data necessary to calculate the degrees and signs on each house cusp for a given birth time and place.

TAI CHI. Ancient Chinese exercise promoting health and longevity.

TRADITIONAL CHINESE MEDICINE. Ancient Chinese medical practice.

T-SQUARE. In astrology, a configuration consisting of two planets in opposition and a third planet that makes a square aspect to both the other planets.

VEDIC ASTROLOGY. Ancient Indian astrology.

VERNAL EQUINOX. The equinox during March.

WHITE DWARF. When the red giant finishes its helium, its core blows its outer layer and contracts into a white dwarf.

YANG. Male energy of chi.

YIN. Female energy of chi.

YOGA. Ancient Indian exercise promoting mental and physical health benefit.

ZODIAC. A group of celestial bodies (constellation) that lies within 7 to 8 degrees on either side of the ecliptic.